WHERE HAVE ALL THE GOOD MEN GONE?

WHERE HAVE ALL THE GOOD MEN GONE?

ISBN-13: 978-0-578-94762-4

WHERE HAVE ALL THE GOOD MEN GONE?

TIFFANY LYN

Contents

- PREFACE -

I can't tell you how many times I've had conversations related to the state of men, relationships and dating these days. Maybe it's a fantasy kindled by romance movies and novels, but chivalry as it's displayed on screens and pages is practically dead. If there are still good men out there, it seems as if they are an endangered species. There are blogs, videos, and courses even on how to find a man, how to keep a man, how to train a man and how to get over a man. The common theme in these renderings is the *man*, but rarely do they talk about the criteria for discerning the virtues of a good man. And if the conversation discusses what being a "good" man means, the vantage point from which it's discussed is questionable at best.

Many of my friends tell me that I'm crazy, insinuating that I live in a fantasy world. They suggest that I will have better luck finding a polka dotted, flying unicorn before getting a man who is loyal, responsible, hardworking, God honoring and loving. "Don't hold your breath or waste your time," they tell me. I would agree if I were looking for a placeholder of the male species, one that can come home every night, eat dinner with me, talk about the day, maybe watch a show or read a book together. With this type of man, he is physically present but may be mentally and emotionally absent. And there is a high probability that there are other women in his DMs who also get this time and attention; but it's "okay", because he's mine.

This has almost become the baseline expectation from a man- that he merely shows up, text here and again and if you're lucky, he may even take you on a date and not expect you to pay for it later, if you get my drift. If this is the standard of what it is to be a good man, then my friends are right when it comes to my standards. I might as well not waste my time or hold my breath.

One thing about me is that I've always been a dreamer. I set goals and push the limits, despite what anyone has to say. You tell me I can't; I'll show you I can. You tell me it's impossible; I'll prove to you that it's inevitable. I got shook for a season when met with some pretty major life disappointments and setbacks. I started to limit myself, first in my thinking and then in my actions. And then one day I woke up and was looking for myself. It was like a surreal moment of hide and seek. I had to go through the reel in my mind, delve through trauma, and find the trash bin where I threw away my hope, tenacity and confidence.

Recently I was listening to a podcast, and the host made a statement that really stood out to me. He said sometimes you have to remember who you are, like *really* remember who you are. I'm simplifying his statement, of course. But this statement so resonated with me. It was a Selah moment, a time to press pause and reflect. I want you to do the same. Take yourself back to a moment when you felt like a Queen, a BOSS, a Treasure. These are not temporal states; these are inherent characteristics. Sweetheart, you *are* the cat's meow. You *are* the epitome of beauty. Your strength is a force to be reckoned with. And if you don't know this or have forgotten this, here is a PSA: *You are amazingly divine.*

You may be thinking, *yeah, this sounds good; it's a nice little cheerleading moment.* But in actuality, it's who you *really* are! When mankind was created, we were made in the image of God Himself. Our intellect, capacity to create and ability to love was all fashioned after Him. When you look at the sunset and think its beauty has no words, that is only a glimmer of the beauty inside of you. We watch the birds that migrate every year as the seasons change. They have this instinct that drives them to the most suitable environment. I always look in amazement and think, "How cool is that? They just know when it's time to go." But isn't it even more astounding that when we know our identity and can be in tune with God's voice, we are capable of doing unfathomable things.

Over time of study and personal experience, I will say that I've gained insight that helps to navigate this arena of doing life with people, so much so that I want to share it with you. And maybe some of the questions and frustration that you've had along the way will be replaced with answers and joyful expectation in knowing that chivalry isn't dead. The positive characteristics of the male species are not extinct, and indeed, all the good men aren't gone.

- 1 -

The Perfect Compliment

Good morning, gorgeous. You look so nice today. Has anyone told you that you have the most amazing walk? Every time you leave, I can't wait for you to return. Do these lines sound familiar? I could go on, but I'm sure you have a list of compliments you've received. The ones that you hear when first getting to know someone, the "Good morning, Queen" texts, and "How was your day, Mami." It's not too much to be redundant and just enough to make you smile. Yes, the perfect compliment to start and end each day.

Let me tell you, I've known some smooth talkers. They could string those words together more beautifully than a Pandora bracelet. I would feel like I was on cloud nine after that text or brief convo. Why? Because the words were directed towards me, and I believed them to be true. Basically, direction and belief were the culprits. If those words had been said to someone else, I probably would have felt happy for the person who received them. It would have been an, "Awe, that's so sweet" kind of thing, no different than the feelings I get when I watch a good romantic comedy. But when it's pointed in my direction, the feeling is more giddy than just happy. Instead of those words being a part of someone else's love story, they become a part of mine. It just hits differently, you know.

Now as far as belief. This element is equally important. The words expressed can be sweeter than honey, but if I don't believe them, then it's like the perfect melody falling on deaf ears. There has to be either established trust or an expectation of genuineness. I like you enough and you've shown up consistently to the point where I can give the benefit of the doubt that you mean what you say. Later on, we'll talk about when we receive words only with no action, but for now let's assume that the compliments are coming from a good place.

So, what do you do when day after day he keeps showing up with the "Hey, gorgeous" and "Yes, Queen" responses? What happens when all he can do is sing your praises, and his voice is so loud that you don't hear anything else? It's almost as if the rest of your senses have gone numb. It doesn't matter that he's past the age of maturity, able bodied but doesn't have a job. Or better yet, he doesn't have a problem getting a job, but it appears it's difficult for him to keep one. Maybe the job isn't the issue. He may not have any interpersonal relationships, no real friends, and the family that lives around the corner is estranged. He doesn't connect with people, because he says people just don't understand him, or he likes to keep to himself. No one gets him like you do. That's what he tells you.

Every hiccup in his life has an explanation, and miraculously, you are the solution. He may even say that God answered his prayer by bringing you into his life. Point being, everything directed towards you is a compliment. You like the way it makes you feel. And you believe both the words and the feeling to be true.

Nothing is wrong with being celebrated and complimented. We should celebrate one another. And certainly in a romantic context, it's imperative to speak positively to your other half and esteem one another. But beyond the words, is there a greater purpose? Does the conversation move beyond sunrise and sunset pleasantries? Are there aligned life purposes? Do you know your purpose? Does he know his?

When I talk about the perfect complement, I'm referring to a pairing of shared vision and goals. Not just surface level stuff like what city to live in or who's going to handle the budget. Yes, those are significant discussion topics, but they aren't destiny shapers or shifters. I'm talking about going beyond what is seen on TV relationship goals. Does your God-given purpose align with theirs? We humans get confused. God does not. He's not going to pair you with someone who isn't even headed in the same direction. The words may even sound good, and the guy may mean them, but what good is a thriller sound bite paired with a comedy clip. Not only does it not fit, it doesn't make sense. And instead of one complimenting the other, the pairing actually takes away from the greatness of both.

So, this begs the question of whether you know your God given purpose. What is that thing that burns inside and keeps you up at night? What do you have a desire to change or to make better? Is there a cause or a project you consistently revisit in numerous seasons of life? The answer to these questions can provide some insight into what God possibly wants you to do. This may or may not be associated with your occupation. And it also may just be a small fragment of the grand scheme of your destiny.

It's important to remember that you don't have to figure it out, your purpose, that is. Before time was a thing, God knew you. He knew every intricate detail about your life - the sound of your voice, how you laugh when something is really funny, what makes you sad, the very number of hairs on your head. Not only does He know you inside and out, He also perfects the details concerning you. Everything in life – the good, the bad, the unexpected – is fashioned and shaped to ultimately work in your favor. As we both know, life is no cakewalk. It sometimes feels like an all out battle. But those battles have a guaranteed outcome and they make us more resilient.

What if you are at a place where you don't know your purpose? Or maybe you are unsure because life has not panned out the way you expected, and you may be wondering did you miss God somewhere. One of the things I love most about God's character is that He doesn't gaslight you. He's not about confusion. If you have a question, His ears are attuned to listen. Not only does He listen, but He also says that He gives us wisdom freely. Nowadays "free" seems to be a foreign concept. There is usually some collateral or stipulation associated with what's being offered. But God's legit. If He says it's free, then it costs you *nothing*. So, if you find yourself in a place of uncertainty, apathy or pure frustration, ask God for clarity. Ask Him to bring His thoughts into your world and realm of understanding.

The process of seeking God can be as simple as this: "Father, thank you for loving me, bringing me close to you and having a plan and purpose for my life. You are so intentional and careful when it comes to me. Align my thoughts with yours, refresh my mind so I can see things clearly, the way you see them. Allow my heart to burn for you, the people and things you have assigned to my life. This day, direct my steps. Give me vision and the will to execute. I want to walk with you today, tomorrow, and the next. In Jesus Name. Amen"

This is a simple prayer that you can communicate to God anytime, every day if you like. And He may give you a big picture of something to do or He may give subtle promptings throughout the day: to call someone, create something, share an idea, make a surprise visit. The essential component is the relationship that you have with Him. If you are a believer in Jesus and you have invited Him into your life, He treasures that fellowship and wants to do life with you. I mean isn't that why we seek relationships, to do life with someone? Well, He desires to do life with you and in the most loving and intimate way. This means the closer you get to Him, the more you spend time with Him, the more you know Him and what He desires.

Intimacy with God is the building block of our identity, our purpose, and subsequently, our partnerships. Understanding the importance of aligned purpose and vision between you and the person of interest truly matters. Why? Because who you pair yourself with or yoke with will either bring you closer to God, your purpose, and your destiny, or it will take you further away. A very beautiful and wise woman told me that marriage is ultimately about purpose, not preference. When you start to see a man in that light, it removes the pressure, resolves insecurity and decision making becomes more resolute. In a few conversations, you can see what's inside a man just by listening to what's said. Does his heart and vision for his life match yours?

There used to be a memory card game. Where there are 50 to 100 tiles with images on them. You start the game by turning over two tiles to see if they match. If they don't match then you turn them face down again and try to make another guess of two different tiles that you hope will match. The idea is that the more tiles you turn over, you'll eventually start to make matches because you remember the images associated with the tiles that were not correctly matched earlier. As I chuckle inwardly, I'm not saying that men are like these tiles, and we should test them out one by one until we find the first match. In this analogy, I liken the tiles to our principles and God-given values. As you are getting to know someone, you start to see his character. You glean what's important to them. You see how they treat people and how they interact with loved ones. That person also gets to see those things about you. And with time, the more tiles or objects of one's character are revealed, it becomes more apparent if those tiles or values are matching up to our own.

The idea here is to have numerous value pairings when it comes to the things that truly matter, which is God's nature and heart. If we understand this, we can more easily identify counterfeits that don't have God's heart and will not be able to love us to the standard that God has deemed best for us. We are going to delve more into God's character. But for now, write down the things you desire that pertain to the character of a man. After you have the list, go back and identify what God says about each one of those traits? If there are any line items that need to be modified or removed, change them. Once again, aligning our thoughts with what God says produces God's best in our lives.

Okay, now that we have touched on aligned purpose, let's discuss how the package looks.

Reflect

You formed my innermost being, shaping my delicate inside and my intricate outside, and wove them all together in my mother's womb.

I thank you, God, for making me so mysteriously complex! Everything you do is marvelously breathtaking. It simply amazes me to think about it! How thoroughly you know me, Lord!

Psalms 139:13-14 TPT

We have become his poetry, a re-created people that will fulfill the destiny he has given each of us, for we are joined to Jesus, the Anointed One. Even before we were born, God planned in advance our destiny and the good works we would do to fulfill it!

Ephesians 2:10 TPT

Reflect

And we know that God causes everything to work together for the good of those who love God and are called according to his purpose for them. For God knew his people in advance, and he chose them to become like his Son, so that his Son would be the firstborn among many brothers and sisters. And having chosen them, he called them to come to him. And having called them, he gave them right standing with himself. And having given them right standing, he gave them his glory.

What shall we say about such wonderful things as these? If God is for us, who can ever be against us? Since he did not spare even his own Son but gave him up for us all, won't he also give us everything else?

Romans 8:28 - 32 NLT

If you don't know what you're doing, pray to the Father. He loves to help. You'll get his help, and won't be condescended to when you ask for it. Ask boldly, believingly, without a second thought. People who "worry their prayers" are like wind-whipped waves. Don't think you're going to get anything from the Master that way, adrift at sea, keeping all your options open.

James 1:5-8 MSG

- 2 -

Dont Judge A Book

I was having a conversation with a friend that I have known for over twenty years, and I was communicating my trepidation in getting to know someone. I was concerned that I would need to let my boundaries be clearly known upfront, as to not waste anyone's time or perpetuate an expectation that would not be met. Her response to me was, "Tiff, don't judge a book by its cover. You may meet someone who unbeknownst to you has the same values and principles. But if you think that just because you didn't meet him in a small group that he doesn't have a close relationship with God, then you may be mistaken. You like to dance Salsa. A guy may think that because you take these classes, you don't have a close relationship with God. You just never know, Tiff, until you know," she said.

Her perspective on the issue got me thinking. Here I am very open minded to height, shades of color, lines of work, but in this particular area, I was limiting myself around the concept of celibacy. I was nervous that I would experience someone that would disrespect my boundaries. Or in this swipe right, swipe left mindset that now exists, I would encounter someone who has a built-in expectation. The expectation being that after three phone conversations and two dates, it's okay to make a move with my full acceptance. Basically, I was psyching myself out. Why was I doing this? Most people who know me have a general idea about what I value. And I venture to say that if a person spent time getting to know me, they would see what's important to me. And as we discussed before, as those character tiles are uncovered, it would become clear if we match up on certain topics. Also, I was discounting the presence of Holy Spirit. He is my counselor and best friend. There are times when I get this immediate check inside of me, a red flag if you will, to keep walking. There is an instinctual knowing that *this ain't it*! So, I can trust that God will help me to discern who's good for me and who's not, irrespective of where or how we first connect.

There was a guy I talked to for a while, and he was very handsome. He was involved in the community and always willing to lend a hand to others. His words were eloquent and his prayers sounded like a stringed quartet. On the surface, this guy had several of the qualities that I wanted. However, I soon observed his impatience with people. His eloquent speech was lost when he felt offended. Then he became abrasive and disrespectful. With time I started to see a pattern of behavior that did not necessarily match with the initial image portrayed to me, and certainly not one that was portrayed regularly to others. In my mind I kept thinking, "But he goes to church and says that he knows God." I was so confused!

After evaluating the situation, I was able to understand that I attributed my values onto someone else. Because I love God, I pray. Because I love God, I go to church. Because I love God, I'm kind to people. So, I held this belief to be true for others. However, what I learned is that some people are just starting their walk with Christ and may not yet be spiritually mature. I wouldn't give a toddler keys to my car and expect the vehicle not to be wrecked somewhere along the way. Someone who is spiritually immature isn't going to be able to have a multidimensional relationship with you if they don't have an in-depth relationship with God. Even if they have memorized scriptures or can pray the house down, a three-year-old toddler can even recite the words to a book, if it is read to him or her repetitively enough. Transformation over information is what matters. And transformation occurs over time.

If church is like a hospital for the sick, hurting, and dying, I shouldn't be surprised that I find those who are sick, hurting, and dying there. That's what church is for. We all need Christ and were dead spiritually, until we surrendered our life to Him. But when we allow Christ into our lives, He heals the broken heart, patches the wounds and gives us a heart transplant. So, now when we show up to regularly examine our heart condition as well as serve others, it's important to be mindful that everyone has a journey of their own. This means they may not be at a place in their process that is healthy or safe to even try to connect emotionally, and vice versa. Gaining this understanding helped to clear up for me why a person can be at church and still be cold towards me and others. Not to mention, there are those who show up but have no real desire to get well.

As the body has many parts, so does the body of Christ. Without each one, the body does not function to its optimal capacity as it was designed. My aim is to make sure that I am well and whole in Jesus, so that I can best play my part with the other muscles, tissues, ligaments, and organs. I pray for my family of faith, and I hope they pray for me. We are in this life together, preparing for life with Christ forever. This is my primary mindset and expectation when I meet someone. One of my mentors once said, "Not everyone you initially connect with is intended for you to walk with." And what he was saying was that although my heart to help is great, that doesn't mean I have to be in a close relationship to help someone.

Bearing this all in mind, I reframed my thoughts about wanting to be with someone who attends church or maybe even serves, because lots of people attend and serve. My desire is to be with someone who has a heart that's transformed by Christ. Not to be displayed with a litany of words, or "good deeds" but with a heart of love and a character that matches the King's. Yes, this type of man would be a match for me, a book I could read cover to cover.

I have another friend who likes tall guys. She's 5'9 and feels some type of way about a man that sees eye to eye with her, literally. Ironically, the person in her life now isn't 6'3; he's 5'10. Super funny guy, charismatic, compassionate, entrepreneurial, a family man, and he treats her exceptionally well. She told me that she never really looked at him with much interest, because she always thought he was too short. But I guess once she cracked open the book and started reading the pages, she began to see that their stories could possibly intertwine. The story is still being read, but it would be a sad tale if she decided to put the book down prematurely, because the font size wasn't her preference. In actuality, it could be the second greatest story ever told.

Attraction is very important and it's not something to be discounted. However, it is only a component of the romance, compatibility and sustainability equation. Have you ever met someone who was *Fine Fine*? I mean they should be on the cover of a magazine type fine? Then maybe from a distance or even personal exchange, the things the person did and said were so off putting? The ego was out of this world. That person was down right mean. And they thought nothing of it, if they hurt or disrespected someone. As the old adage goes, beauty is only skin deep. It's okay to start with the appearance, but that can't be the ending point. We have to dig deeper. Just because something is packaged nicely, it doesn't mean its contents won't be destructive.

TNT, even in a box with a bow, will still blow you up.

I'm sure you've probably had some life experiences to which you can relate. One time I went to an auction to purchase a car for my then boyfriend (I know, horrible idea). The outside of the car was decent. The interior did not have any tears. And the engine sounded good. So, I purchased the car. But not too long after I drove it off the lot, it stopped working. I had it towed to my mechanic, and he told me that it would need a major repair. I was so disappointed. I felt bamboozled. The car sounded good. It looked good. It even fit into my budget. And someone sold it to me. I would think they would have disclosed any irregularities with the car before allowing someone to buy it. NOPE! I was now the owner of a car that could not do what a car was designed to do, get me safely and efficiently from point A to point B.

This is what happens when we buy into the exterior of a man only, what he looks like, sounds like, what he does for a living, etc. On the outside, it can look really good! He can be very well established in his profession, own a home, have an investment portfolio, yet he can also be someone who is self-absorbed, narcissistic, abusive, controlling. You just don't know unless you take the time to look under the hood and invite someone who is qualified to provide an accurate assessment of the state of being.

God's not going to lead you wrong. So if you come across someone who expresses interest, and they mutually pique your interest on the exterior qualities, then invite God into the situation. He may endorse it and say yes, this person is someone who should be in your life and then let you know in what capacity. Or He may say, "Nah, don't do that." Because God knows as soon as you drive off the lot and get your feelings involved whether that relationship is going to break down and leave you stranded on the side of the road. And to make matters worse, not only did the person not treat you well, but now you're having to have major repair work done on your mind, emotions and soul. Don't let the exterior fool you. Otherwise, you may find yourself in a situation where a man shows up promising to take you around the world, but he under delivers by barely taking you down the block. Simply put, the inside must match the outside.

Reflect

But God told Samuel, “Looks aren’t everything. Don’t be impressed with his looks and stature. I’ve already eliminated him. God judges persons differently than humans do. Men and women look at the face; God looks into the heart.”

1 Samuel 16:7 MSG

- 3 -

Red Flags

Have you ever had a moment when you said, *why didn't I just follow my gut?* I certainly have. Like caution lights on the road or a stop sign, there's usually an indicator in situations and relationships where we see a signal that we may need to slow down, pause, evaluate and possibly make a U-turn to change our course of direction. As my dad likes to say often, "Tiffany, when someone shows you who they are, believe them."

In hindsight, I will say this is one of the biggest mistakes that I've made, relationally. Through reflection and even counseling, I've learned why I made some of those decisions or mistakes. One of my dreams growing up was to get married shortly after graduating from college and start a family. My husband and I would have a house, a couple of kids, and a big backyard for weekend barbeques. There would be two vacations every year, one for the entire family during the summer and one a little later, just for me and my man.

Well, where did these dreams and thoughts come from? When I was a kid, I remember my friends would come back from spring break or summer vacation and talk about where their families went and all of the fun things they did. I would think to myself, "Boy, I would love to do that one day." Instead of my reality of traveling to Dublin, Georgia, in my dreams, I'd pack up my family and fly to Dublin, Ireland. It wasn't the extravagance that appealed to me, it was creating a unique, unforgettable experience.

I must say creating a unique, unforgettable experience was exactly what happened. I got married in college one semester before graduating. I'd been dating for two and a half years, and I was tremendously in love and so excited about my future. I was graduating with honors from business school. Employment was lined up, and I was planning to go back to get my master's degree shortly thereafter.

Everything looked like it was going according to plan, if I continued to excuse the red flags. During that dating season, there were signs that I blatantly ignored. I had a vision in my mind of what I wanted my life to look like, and I did not allow for the hands and voice of God to direct me on the best path for my life, as He will do for us. And being that God is the gentleman, He's not going to impose or force His will upon mine. Just like how I have to choose Him to be Lord of my life, I also have to choose to follow Him daily. Maybe if I had been a little more patient, maybe if I had not made certain internal vows that I was going to have this great dynamic family. If I had not been so invested in the hope that it was going to wipe away some of the things that I experienced growing up, I may have been able to be more sensitive to Holy Spirit and make a different choice that would have ultimately changed the course of my life.

As my story goes, I did get married. I had four children and ended up getting a divorce eleven years into the marriage. This was extremely devastating for me. I always saw myself as a wife, never as a divorcee. I saw myself having a life partner, never being a single mother. Where did I go wrong? I checked off all the boxes of what I thought I was supposed to do to make love last and a marriage work. But there I was, faced with a shattered dream and the reality of a failed marriage, like so many others.

I'd like to stop here and tell you that this divorce was a shifting point in my story. I'd learned so much about interpersonal relationships. I'd even gone back to school and studied marriage and family therapy. Even prior to being married, I had a passion to help others become healthy individuals and create sustainable family structures. However, in the course of learning so much about human dynamics, the one thing I failed to address was my willful disregard of red flags. This was evident in my next relationship and subsequent marriage. And guess what, just like the first marriage, the second did not last. Both were for completely different reasons, but both failed surrounding the red flags I saw when we were dating.

Part of identifying what is good is understanding what is not. There truly are wonderful men who are fathers, brothers, neighbors, coworkers, and yes, a life partner for you. There are also men who are growing and working on themselves and just aren't ready for high-level commitment, because God is still working on them. God is transforming His sons to best exhibit His character. Then there are other men who just aren't open to being changed by God. With this group, it's best to just stay away. Pray for them, yes, but date them . . . no. Well, how do you best tell which group a man may belong to? Glad you asked. Pay attention, do not ignore and carefully assess *all* the red flags.

Red flags are indicators of potential hazardous conditions down the road. When a meteorologist forecasts the weather and believes the temperature may drop below freezing, a freeze warning is issued. If they believe a tornado could form, a tornado warning is rendered. If you see red flags, this is an indicator that an ice storm or wind raging at 120 mph could be headed your way. Failure to observe and take precautionary measures when forewarned could result in severe losses, not just in the natural when it comes to weather but the same is true also in relationships.

Let me give some examples: If a man is lying to you and cheating on you while you are dating, there is a high probability that he will do the same and even more after you are married. Some of you may say, "We were young when we met, and he made mistakes that he learned from and hasn't exhibited this behavior sense." And if this is your story, that's awesome! He took the time to work on that area and chose to value you and your relationship. However, there are scenarios where there is not a change in behavior. And the decisions we make, especially repeated decisions, reflect something going on within. To change the outside, there needs to be a shift that occurs on the inside. That shift comes from a genuine encounter with Jesus. We all have a desire to do better in certain areas, but without Holy Spirt empowering us, encouraging us, and holding us accountable, it's not sustainable. That's why a daily relationship with God is so important. We can clearly hear His voice and are willing to obey whatever He says. Also, being in community that will hold us accountable is imperative. I'm not referring to the coworkers you may share stories with or even that cousin you add as your plus one to every event. I'm talking about the women who pray with you and for you and will say what God says, whether you like it or not. They will hold us to the standard of what we say we believe and desire to live out.

What about disrespect? If a man is disrespectful to you in any way, then that *is* a red flag. If he makes jokes about you and it makes you feel uncomfortable, you don't like the way it makes you feel. If he responds with telling you that you are being too sensitive or says he didn't really mean it that way, yet he continues to make the same comments and jokes, that's disrespectful and a form of gaslighting. He's trying to get you to doubt your sense of reality and to believe that you're the issue. It's your sensitivity and not his disrespectful nature that's the problem. If a man is easily angered, yells at you, is very abrasive towards you, gives you the silent treatment or stone walls you, those are red flags. If he starts to break or throw things or drives crazy on the freeway when he becomes angry, these are red flags. Yes, I do understand that it's easy to empathize with someone who has experienced a broken childhood, fatherlessness, motherlessness or other difficulties in life. However, empathy does not mean that you have to be in a relationship with someone who needs to clearly work through these things. And these issues need to be worked through on their own, not with you as a conduit to their disrespect and ill-treatment. You alone cannot be their support system, even if they say you are the only one who cares.

Another dynamic you may encounter is a person who does not have very many friends or is somewhat estranged from family. This may be a red flag, if the people closest to them don't want to be around them. There's probably a back-story there. That's not to say that a man who doesn't have a very close relationship with his family is a bad guy. It may be that the family is toxic, and he's created distance to protect himself. However this dynamic is something that requires careful evaluation, processing and prayer. A few other red flags are: excessive drinking or substance abuse, an inability to sustain a job or manage money, or dependent living with family for an extended period of time.

Overlooking red flags in the dating phase is costly. For me, I saw inappropriate text messages and phone conversations, infidelity, disrespect, passive-aggressive behavior, anger and bouts of silent treatment. I attributed these various actions to a broken childhood. Maybe they needed me to understand them and to just love them into a better place. This way of thinking was 100% wrong. My issue was codependency, wanting to love and be loved. Despite any brokenness experienced in life, Jesus is the lover my soul. He is the healer. He is the sustainer. No one can be God to me, and I can't be God to someone else. It's not our job as women to fix a man. That's God's department. Individual work has to be done on both sides before a relationship is formed, otherwise there could be serious collateral damage.

There are all types of red flags and, as my counselor once said to me, "Tiffany, you can't take a red flag and paint a different picture and say, 'look at the beautiful sunset with all the red and orange in the background'." That's how I treated red flags, like they were there, but part of painting, a beautiful picture that I could grow to love and appreciate and honestly desire. I maximized the minimal and minimized the dominant behaviors that were being displayed in the relationship. And if I could take it a step further and be a little more transparent, I would tell you that I saw the flags even *before* I was in a relationship with people in my past. There were things that I observed in our first few conversations, or even in conversations with their family, that should have been places of pause for me.

That being said, I want to affirm that you're not being paranoid; it's okay to ask questions. No, you don't have to interrogate someone on a first or second date, but if you listen closely, you'll get an idea of some things that you should start praying about and develop some questions that you want to ask God. This is part of guarding your heart, which is what God tells us to do. He tells us above all else to guard our hearts, because out of it flows the issues of life.

The hurt that I've experienced and hurts that you may have experienced in a relationship are real. Someone's actions are never your fault. Never, ever, ever . . . But it is your responsibility to be on guard, because your heart is so valuable. Allow Holy Spirit to speak very clearly to you and do whatever He says, no matter how cute a guy is, no matter how successful, no matter how funny and charming he may be. Man looks at the outside, but God looks at the heart. And because God can see beyond the skin's surface, we have to invite Him into the conversation for direction.

Should you feel bad about having to walk away after maybe investing significant time getting to know someone? Absolutely not! If someone is not good to you and if someone is not good for you, then it is not only okay, but it is wise to distance oneself from that situation. This doesn't mean that it has to be awkward between you and that individual; it can actually be very amicable. However, God tells us if someone is hot-tempered, to not associate with individuals like that. He tells us also that bad company corrupts good character. So, if someone is lying, being deceptive, manipulative, or exhibiting characteristics that are not Christ-like then that's the time to listen to what God says about stepping away from that relationship. It may be for a season or maybe indefinitely; Holy Spirit will let you know. But stepping away is what God tells us to do in those situations so that we can indeed protect our hearts.

One of my friend's nana would often say, "Your first thought is your right thought." If you have a feeling about a person or a situation, don't ignore it. You can trust yourself. Despite what anyone may have told you or tried to get you to believe, your feelings, including your intuition, is God given. You know when something doesn't feel right. These are your feelings, your safety zone. Honor them.

I've come a long way, as it relates to dealing with red flags. I no longer paint a beautiful sky of birds flying in the distance. I can see a situation for what it is and am confident enough in my God-given value to be okay with saying, this dynamic is not serving me well or working for me. Maybe at one point it did, but it no longer does. This does not suggest that people are dispensable by any means. However, relationships are meant to be edifying. If you aren't building me up and if I'm not building you up, then what is the point of us being in relationship with one another? If there is confusion, anger, strife, sadness, any type of negative emotion on a regular basis, that is actually deterring not only one person but both individuals from fully accomplishing their purpose on this Earth.

Sometimes it's not about one person being the bad guy and the other person being the good guy. Sometimes two people just can't walk together. I remember the story in the Bible where Abraham and his cousin Lot were on a mission that God had given Abraham. But as they traveled, the people in the respective camps began to fight. As a result, a decision was made for Lot to pick an area of land that he wanted to settle in with his group of people. Then Abraham would pick another area where he would settle with his group of people. Once decided, they went their separate ways, so that the purpose God had originally ordained for Abraham's life could continue to go forward.

Wherever there is strife and dissension, it inhibits God's ability to work. Yes, God is sovereign. Yes, God is powerful. Yes, God can do anything. The atmosphere through which God works is not one of confusion. That's not His character. So, sometimes even good people have to go their separate ways and no longer walk together, because it is not allowing them to show up as their best selves. And if something or someone is unhealthy, you're losing weight, losing sleep, can't keep any food down, there's abuse going on, you're constantly questioning yourself, you're in a state of dysphoria, you have to get away from that as quickly and as safely as possible. You have to get away from any type of situation that puts your life, or physical mental, emotional, spiritual well-being at risk, ASAP.

The first and greatest command is to love God. And then we are to love our neighbors as ourselves. The first part seems pretty obvious ... to love God. He's number one. And all this really entails is putting Him first and considering what He says is best, over what we think is best. It's being able to lay down what you want and picking up what He desires. This may seem like a very foreign concept, but it's actually a very beautiful thing when you understand the heart and nature of God. God's thoughts and plans are a million times better than anything that you or I can ever imagine. And that's a promise that He's made. When you're in love with God, just like in real life, you pick up when He calls. If He asks you to do something, your heart is eager to make Him smile. Writing a book, leaving a job, starting a new venture isn't an arduous task, when you're in love. Whatever He's instructing you to do is part of His divine plan for you to not only honor Him but also to impact others. It's so important to just trust God, step out on faith and follow Him.

After loving God, the next thing He asks us to do is to love your neighbor as yourself. For the longest time, I did not really focus on "as yourself." I focused on loving other people. So, I was constantly pouring out into others, who in my relationships, had no problems accepting everything I was willing to give. Financially, emotionally, logistically, you name it. If you needed me, I'd show up. I would invent ways of how to be unique in loving a person, based on what I gleaned mattered to them most. But in all of this, I lost loving myself. I loved people who were abusive towards me. And not only did I love them, I stayed in relationships with them, which allowed the abuse to continue.

The self-love component of this command is essential. Reason being, when you see red flags and you realize they could be detrimental to you, the part where you are to love yourself will kick in. You will be able to step back from that situation and show up for yourself the way you were willing to constantly show up for others. It's the perfect opportunity to pray for the other person, while remaining in a space of fatherly and self-love. So from here on out, when you see red flags, don't ignore them. The love for you is too great, your value is too high, and your purpose too indispensable.

Reflect

So above all, guard the affections of your heart, for they affect all that you are. Pay attention to the welfare of your innermost being, for from there flows the wellspring of life.

Proverbs 4:23 TPT

Do not be misled: "Bad company corrupts good character."

1 Corinthians 15:33 NIV

Lot, who was traveling with Abram, was also rich in sheep and cattle and tents. But the land couldn't support both of them; they had too many possessions. They couldn't both live there—quarrels broke out between Abram's shepherds and Lot's shepherds. The Canaanites and Perizzites were also living on the land at the time.

Abram said to Lot, "Let's not have fighting between us, between your shepherds and my shepherds. After all, we're family. Look around. Isn't there plenty of land out there? Let's separate. If you go left, I'll go right; if you go right, I'll go left."

Genesis 13:5 - 9 MSG

Reflect

“Teacher, which is the most important commandment in the law of Moses?”

Jesus replied, “‘You must love the Lord your God with all your heart, all your soul, and all your mind.’ This is the first and greatest commandment. A second is equally important: ‘Love your neighbor as yourself.

Matthew 22:36 - 39 NLT

- 4 -

Qualities Of A Good Man

Now that you know the qualities you don't want and what signs to look out for, what are the qualities of a good man that should be present? The answer to this question can vary from one individual to the next, based on upbringing, cultural background and personal experience. The answer may also change based on which generation you're part of. What one generation values may be completely different from what another generation values. And it makes sense for the answer to be highly individualized, because this is your relationship. You're the one who's going to have to live with this person, ideally forever. This is why it is important to have the qualities that you desire in a mate, because they are going to be your life partner. Interestingly, you will love over multiple decades and seasons of life. So the core qualities must be sustainable and adaptable to inevitable seasons of change.

One characteristic I love about God is that He is immutable. This means that He does not change. There are multiple times and places in the scripture where He says that He does not change or shift like shadows. What He says, His word will accomplish. He doesn't change His mind. And the reason why I love this characteristic about God is it means that I can trust Him. He doesn't say one thing one day and then within the next 15 - 20 minutes say He was just kidding or that's not really what He meant. This type of double talk would leave your entire world topsy-turvy, because you put your weight on a set of criteria based on what He said in His promises. No, God's not like that. If He said it, He will do it. When you know that you can count on something, then you can build your life on it. And do you know what the coolest thing is? We have Holy Spirit with us every day. God with us is fulfilling His word in our lives day in and day out. Because of this trustworthiness in God's character, the qualities of a good man are what *God says* the qualities of a good man should be. And if God says something is good, you can trust it.

In the beginning, God created the world through His words. He said let there be light and there was light. He continued to speak and created the day and the night, carving land and separating it from the water's edge. Species of plants and animals were made. Then God made man in His own likeness and He said that His creation was good, very good.

From the beginning of time, the creation of man is seen

by God to be good even before a woman was fashioned. God is Holy and cannot lie. So this gives us confidence in knowing and believing that man is good. Trust me, I've had numerous times where I've wanted to question God on this point. These were moments where I have said, "Lord, did you see what your son just did? He is over here tripping and talking to me like he's crazy. I don't know what's possessed him, but he does not look like You right now!" Yes, I've asked God on occasion what's up with your creation, because You said this was good and if it's so good, why is this man over here acting a fool?

It's not that the creation isn't good, it's the heart condition that impacts how the creation chooses to operate. If you continue to read the story of creation in Genesis, you see how the fall of man occurs and how the world shifts into chaos. God loves us so much that He gave us a choice of whether we are going to love Him, walk with Him and serve Him. I don't know anybody, or I should say a healthy person, who wants to be in a relationship with someone they have to force to be with them. They have to force a person to call and hang out with them, to be kind to them, to care even. That is exhausting. If I have to make you do something to show that you like me or care, then that's just not for me.

God in His love and kindness gave us free will to choose Him or to not choose Him. This is so beautiful about the relational dynamic of God. The Father, Jesus, and Holy Spirit are complete within themselves. They did not *need* to make mankind, but they wanted to. The Bible says before the world existed, He chose us. It is our choice whether or not we choose Him back. It's a heart condition, a choice that is made within the core or soul of a person of how they're going to react to the ultimate life choice that God has given to us. The choice is to choose Him and walk with Him or to eternally exist apart from Him.

How does this tie into the qualities of a good man? Well, someone who has a heart surrendered to Christ understands a life of commitment. When you love someone, you desire to please them. You don't desire to do things to hurt their heart in any way. You're not perfect, but when you make a mistake, you quickly apologize, acknowledge it and you try your very best to do better. As you walk with a person over time, you get to know them and understand their character. You build a life of experiences together. You love them. And doing so creates a space where you both can simultaneously love on one another. So when you find someone, the determining factor of goodness is based on him exemplifying God's character.

This means that good men do exist. Not just in the general sense of the creation. But good in the sense that they have accepted Christ and are allowing Him to transform them daily. They live a life surrendered to God. There are men in this day, time and age who are committed to this kind of love and life. We know this because God says that we are a royal priesthood, a chosen generation. This means that in every generation, as long as the Earth has been and long as it will ever be, there are a group of people, both men and women, who have a heart and passion for Christ. They seek to uphold the standard of what it means to love as God commands us to love.

This begs the question of what does love look like? Well, we know from 1 Corinthians that love is patient, kind, not boastful or proud, forgives, always hopes, perseveres and never gives up. I know if you've read the scripture or heard this before, it may just seem like background noise. Contrarily, this is the essence of what interpersonal relationships should look like. God is love and since His Spirit lives within us, we have the capacity to be transformed by His Spirit so that we love like He loves. Our entire design and makeup is to be a reflection and an image of Christ, God the Father, and Holy Spirit. Think about it; for God so loved the world that He gave His only son. And over time we see countless interactions in the Bible and throughout history of hundreds of thousands of encounters, where mankind has rebelled against what God divinely wants for us. And we see Him show up the same. He is patient, and He doesn't remember wrongs against us. He always hopes for the best in us. Through everything that we go through, His love never fails.

On a day-to-day basis God's love should be exemplified in and through us. As mentioned, this does not mean to forsake self-love, and it does not mean perfection. If we were perfect, we wouldn't need Jesus. However, our aim is to love like He does. Therefore, one of the characteristics and qualities of a good man is that he loves like God loves. He should be patient, kind, gentle, not self-serving, nor boastful, forgiving and has stick-to-itiveness.

There's a lot that we can dissect as it pertains to what love looks like, and I think it's worth unpacking just to have this clarity. This is especially necessary, because you may have had one or two examples of what it does *not* look like. Love is to be patient. We all know what patience means. Patience is the willingness to work through a situation, to be responsive and not reactive in a harsh or negative way. To maintain a graceful countenance, while working through internal or external circumstances exemplifies patience. A life partner needs to be able to weather the storms of life with you. Those tempests could be emotional, physical, or financial in nature. Either way, a man that is patient is not going to treat you differently, because life is happening around you and you may be struggling to navigate the moment. He is going to consistently show up, while you go through that situation.

Love is also kind, and kindness is king. I cannot emphasize enough how important it is to have someone in your life who can exemplify kindness. And don't take it for granted. Sometimes we may presume that kindness is innate within a human being, but that's not necessarily the case. Depending on where you grew up and how your family dynamics played out, a man might not be kindhearted by nurture. It may be something that he needs to develop before entering into a relationship. But he should be a kind person. He should be sweet, gentle, and tender. If he doesn't like or understand something, his default should be gentleness.

Gentleness is another part of the love dynamic. There is a time and place for everything. Your relationship is not a sporting match, so there should be no need to scream and yell at you. He should not pull you around or wrestle with you, like you're another man. Nor should he speak to you like you are one of his bros. You're his woman, so he needs to honor your delicate nature. You're not fragile or weak by any means. However, a good man realizes that you are a gem, a treasure. And when you have something delicate, let's say an heirloom, you don't just toss it around or treat it haphazardly. You're very careful when you move it from one place to the next. You move with it gingerly. This is the way he is supposed to treat you, with care.

After patience, kindness, and gentleness, we see that love is not puffed up. I'm sure you've had experiences with someone who had a big head. You're in a conversation talking about your day, and this person is yawning as you speak, as if what you're saying is not important. The conversations are usually one-sided and require your full undivided attention, although you do not receive the same. The funny thing is I actually dealt with someone who was like this. If I was sad, this person seemed to be okay with it. But if life was great for me, and I was talking and excited, I would receive from him a huge, mouth wide open, see to the back of his throat type yawn. The nonverbal communication in these moments spoke loudly. The message was, "What you're saying does not matter to me. Your success, highlights and happiness are of little interest." However, he could go on for hours and talk about his day, the things that made him happy and what frustrated him. Love is not self-centered and prideful.

It doesn't find itself consumed with *I, Me*, and *My*. It embraces *We, Ours, You* and *Yours*. Pride is a no go, which is not the same as confidence.

Confidence promotes security. It is one of the qualities of a good man. There's a scripture that says to be strong in the Lord and in the power of His might. God also tells Joshua to be strong and courageous. In numerous instances we see the command to be strong and to be courageous in the Lord. So even if we do feel timid, trepidatious or a little bit hesitant, we can put our confidence in God. A good man is definitely confident. But his confidence is not in his abilities, what he has done, or what he's going to do. His confidence is in God's ruling in his life, guiding and directing him. When confidence is in anything other than God, it leaves room for pride to enter.

Pride is the genesis of original sin and it leads to nowhere very quickly. It says, *I know better than God and can do better than God*. Love, on the contrary, is devoid of pride. Love is humble. It's not afraid to go low.

Jesus said that He did not come to be served but to serve. The fact that He was maker of the entire universe didn't interfere with Him modeling servant leadership. One astounding example is when Jesus washed His disciples' feet. And in my mind, they had to be crusty. I mean the smell alone after a long day of work can literally take one's breath away. I've had to leave my man's shoes in the garage before because they smelled like everything sour left in the sun for 10 days. And the socks, forget about it! They were going directly into the washing machine, once they hit the front door. If you can imagine the disciples walking in open-toe sandals in the dust getting dirty all day long. Now here comes Jesus, the one who made everything we see, God in all His glory, washed what may have been stinky, crusty, calloused feet. This is one of the ultimate expressions of humility. Jesus did not even think about His title.

For another example, let's consider a man's work and how it relates to humility. If you meet a man that's very successful or progressing in his line of work it shows that he has ambition, fortitude, and the ability to provide. He does not have to be at the pinnacle of his career but he should be operable. God says that a man that does not work, does not eat. A woman is to compliment and help along that journey, not drag him into destiny. And sometimes we can do that. We see the potential in a man, and we develop a Build-A-Bear mentality, thinking if we put certain skill sets on him, get him through school, or dress him up a certain way that he's going to miraculously transform into exactly what we wanted. This is problematic, because he may not ascribe to this vision. Not only that, but God is our maker, the one that assigns purpose and fashions what our future looks like. A woman is able to come alongside a man and both walk together in their God-given purpose. Whether he is just starting the journey or well along the way, observe his heart posture.

Sometimes you may see men at the top of their game, very successful professionally, and they come across as arrogant. They're making the type of money they want. They speak to people in a curt way and put you on an internal timer while in their presence. I once had a guy tell me that his time was valuable. So basically, I should feel special that he was willing to talk to me. In my mind, I was like *no he did not!* Everybody's time is valuable, because we only get 24 hours in a day. Once it's spent there are no exchanges. What someone chooses to do with those hours may be wasteful, but the time never loses its value. When you come across the type of people who treat others as less than, pay attention. How someone treats a server, parking attendant or employee can be a sign of how you will be treated. Love is humble. Love does not consider itself better than anybody, but instead is willing to meet the needs of someone else.

So, love is patient. Love is kind. It is gentle. It doesn't have the "big head." Love is not self-seeking. What this means is that a person is not all about themselves and what they want or need. The world does not revolve around them. This trait goes hand in hand with being prideful and puffed up. It's saying love is not selfish. In a relationship or marriage, a person can't be selfish and have it work well. The relationship can't be one-sided; there has to be a give and take. It's not about primarily doing what one person wants. That's why it's so important to be aligned and have some shared interests. Because you can find yourself in a situation where the things you and your partner want to do are polar opposites, which makes it more difficult to compromise.

For example, if a man asked me to jump out of a plane, I may love him deeply, but I'm not jumping out of a plane. I'm not jumping out by myself. I'm not jumping attached to somebody else. I'm not jumping, period. My feet are staying on the ground and if I do go into the air, I will remain inside the aircraft at all times and at all cruising altitudes. I will graciously see him on the ground. But if this is something that is important to him, and he wants a woman to jump off a plane with him, that's just not my guy. I'm just not his girl. And that's okay. However, scenarios where you reach an impasse shouldn't be the norm. Compromise should be the common language of the relationship. If you like painting and he likes sporting events, find a way to incorporate both activities in your time together. One may not be your preference, but you can make compromise a priority. You both choose to show up for one another and are willing to meet a need, even if it's not your own.

The next mile marker of love is that it isn't easily angered. I need to take a pause on this, a moment of silence. Love is not easily angered. So many times and instances in the Bible God warns us about being around hot-tempered people. Blatantly God says don't do it. He says don't hang out with people who fly off the handle on a dime. Why? Because you will become like them and learn their ways, God says. He also tells us that hot tempered people are operating in a mindset of foolishness. They become abnormally upset because somebody cut them off on the freeway, start yelling obscenities, and telling them to pull over. What would happen if they're talking to you and you cut them off prematurely in conversation? What would happen if they're in the process of doing something and you interrupted them?

Responses such as these are indicators of character. And because we are talking about the qualities of a good man, be assured that he's not easily angered. If you do something, he's not going to just start yelling and screaming at you and throwing items. Sad to say and I wish I didn't have that story, but I was with somebody who was easily angered. There may have been some other underlying conditions there, but that doesn't excuse rageful behavior. Literally, we could go from laughing together to me crying, fearful and locking myself in the next room. Couches were being flipped over, tables broken and chairs smashed like it was nothing. An entire room was disintegrated within moments because of a misunderstanding. He would say something; I didn't respond the way he wanted, so then there would be flying off the handle or dangerously speeding on the freeway, because I didn't answer the question "right." On one occasion, the speed was approaching 90 mph, yet while he was driving, he started punching the steering wheel. My thoughts were, "Oh my God, we're going to die. We're going to crash. Someone is going to get hurt."

You may have your own examples from personal experience or through observation. If so, you know that someone who is easily angered is not safe. A healthy man or woman needs to be able to process his or her emotions. They need to be able to think through things. Anger in and of itself is not a sin. But God does caution that in your anger, don't sin. Anger should not turn into rage. It should not turn into screaming matches. It should not turn into an opportunity to be like a Tasmanian devil and just wreck everything around. It shouldn't turn into vindictiveness or seek to punish others. If someone is mad and decides to give you the silent treatment, or turn their back on you while you were in the middle of communicating, this is disrespect. Love does not dishonor others. And the presence of a given emotion cannot be used as an excuse to mistreat someone.

Love is not easily angered. This is so very important, not just for yourself but also if you are considering having a family with someone who doesn't regulate their anger. Children absorb what they see. As an adult, one should be able to process emotions. So, if the kids break something or do something they're not supposed to, the response is one of patience, communication and correction, if needed. Someone who can take a walk to cool off or table a conversation for a later time and commit to revisiting the issue is showing signs of maturity. That is what love looks like - being able to step away and take those moments to deal with the emotion present.

God gave us emotions, so they are not bad. I like the story where Jesus goes into the temple, and those inside were selling things like it was a flea market. Jesus was not having it! He was upset, because that was not supposed to be happening in His Father's house. He shut it down very quickly. So there's nothing wrong with being angry. It's the action, or lack of, which comes after the emotion that matters. Some people choose to give full vent to their anger. And this goes for both men and women. If communication cannot occur without someone being hurt physically or emotionally, then work needs to be done before entering a relationship. God's daughters and sons have to honor one another. And both should exemplify these qualities and characteristics of love.

The next dynamic of love is a doozy. Love keeps no record of wrongs. I don't know about you, but I've had to really work on this one. It's not necessarily bringing up the past in a nasty way. For me it was a protective mechanism. I was in very manipulative relationships. I'd find myself in situations where the other person would communicate that he didn't say something, when he actually did. Or, entire events that transpired would be denied. At that time, to keep track of what was actually happening, I would make sure to remember the details, small and great. This was an issue in and of itself. Honesty is a characteristic of a good man. And if tabs and records need to be kept to validate the authenticity of a story, then that's not someone to be with. It's time to quickly exit stage right.

Love doesn't keep a record of wrongs. When we mess up and ask God to forgive us, He does and chooses not to remember them anymore. As far as the East is from the West, that's how far removed our wrongs are with God. Yeah, that's pretty far! Currently, I live in the United States on the East coast. If I fly to California on the West Coast, that's about a four-hour plane ride. If I took a train or drove across the country, it would take days. Now, imagine that I'm going to another continent around the world. Depending on mode of transportation, it could take days, months even. As far as the East is from the West, that's how much God removes our wrongs from His mind. Obviously, we are not God. We are human, but we are made in His image and we do have His Spirit to help us. Although the memory might not necessarily be erased from the mind, the sting of it is no longer present. There's no longer a reaction.

When I was in high school, I participated in cheerleading. One day at practice we had a water break. As we were returning from break, the coaches started blowing the whistle. Everybody had to be back on the blacktop. With a minute to get in place, everyone started running. All of a sudden several of us fell to the ground. I slid across the ground. My left shoulder was burning. Tears started to stream down my face. My friends tried to distract me from looking at my shoulder. When I finally did, I understood why. All I could see was white meat and blood. The wound was about the size of a silver dollar and it hurt badly.

Over 20 years later, I have the scar on my shoulder from where I slid across the pavement when I was in high school. At the time, it hurt terribly, but now I rarely notice the scar. And when I do see it, it doesn't impact me. It's no longer sore to the touch. It's fine because it's completely healed. The scar is still there, so there's no denying I was injured at some point. That's what it is like to not remember wrongs. You process through the situation. For example, if your man didn't call and he's supposed to be taking you on a date. It's not characteristic of him, but you have made plans and he didn't show up. You talk through it, process through it and you move on from it. You don't live in the place of disappointment or brokenness based on what happened. Although some things take more time than others to process through, at some point you will fully process the pain. That doesn't mean that the event didn't happen. What it means is that it no longer hurts to remember. When it surfaces in your mind, it's a fleeting thought. You're able to just keep it pushing without your countenance being affected. There are traumatic events that occur that may take significant time and support to process. Even in these situations, the way in which you process through them gets progressively better. In year ten, you may not need to have a deep conversation with a person questioning why they did what they did. Acknowledge the feeling and thought, understanding that every situation and healing process is different. Some scabs stay on longer than others. But at some point it does come off. This holds true relationally. You cannot live your entire life bound to *their* wrongdoing. It's not healthy or helpful for you, or them.

We all do and say things we wish we had never done or said. We are not perfect people, so we are going to make mistakes. I certainly don't want to forever be on the hook for all of my wrongs. No one should be held to that standard. God, our creator, who has done no wrong can love and forgive us all the time even when we do the same thing over and over. How much more should we be willing to forgive another? Is it fair to hold someone to a standard that God doesn't hold us to?

Releasing offences is essential in every relationship. That's why this season is very important when you're determining with whom you will share your life. You're going to face challenges. He's going to make you mad, and you're going to make him mad. You'll both be disappointed, but the relationship can't stop thriving and moving forward just because there's disappointment. In this phase of assessing if someone is going to be a good life partner for you, evaluate how well issues are resolved. Are you able to move past disappointment, or are you stuck on an issue that happened in week two of dating?

I remember in one of my relationships I made a big mistake. I called the guy I was currently dating my ex-husband's name in conversation. I was asking for him to pass me the chips, and my brain malfunctioned in that moment and pulled the wrong name out. I'd previously had a long-standing history with my ex-husband, and this relationship was fairly new. I felt horrible and would have completely understood if the person I was dating wanted to walk away. But he chose to continue dating me. When it would come up, I'd acknowledge it and apologize. Months passed and it was still being discussed. It was as if nothing I did or said could outpace my mistake. We all have free will and the beauty of choice. If an interaction or event doesn't sit well, there is the option to be seated at another table. The past does not define a person, and present mistakes are not meant to be an imprisonment. Be willing to forgive and move forward. In the same light, include people in your life who are willing to do the same.

Next we see that love does not rejoice in evil but it upholds truth. At surface level, this is straightforward. If something is wrong, it shouldn't be relabeled as right. It certainly shouldn't be celebrated. But going a bit deeper, what does God say is evil and what is truth? When evaluating the person or people you have in your life in general, you may want to ask yourself, "Is this person encouraging me to pursue God? Are they encouraging me to pursue purpose? Do they even listen to God for themselves?" God has a different standard of right and wrong. Therefore, the people who are in close proximity to you relationally need to be like minded, meaning Christ-centered. Otherwise, when it comes to values and decision-making, there are going to be problems. Will that person respect, support, and even lead you along the right path, because they are committed to the same course.

The condition and commitment of the heart is important. Is their life committed to living out God's truth? Not in a religious way, more so for show or out of a sense of obligation, but instead out of genuine love for God. If there's something going on in the community around them and it doesn't involve them, are they dismissive? Are they sensitive to other economic, cultural or racial groups of people? Are they an advocate for the poor, underserved or maligned? Do they rejoice in truth as God sees and defines it? How about you? This is a great area to invite God into, becoming more sensitive to the needs and experiences of others. As we go deeper in God, we grow more in truth.

The final leg of 1st Corinthians 13 on love reminds us that it protects. It always hopes. It trusts and it perseveres. Love protects; basically, it's a place of faith. So a quality of a good man who is walking in the love of Christ will be his protectiveness of you and others. Inherently when God created man, one of the first assignments received was to tend to the garden. He was to oversee and protect the creation that God made. This is something that man was instructed to do from the very beginning of time. When a woman comes into the picture and Adam says, *this is bone of my bone and flesh of my flesh.* He realizes, "This is me right here!" From the beginning, there is an innate sense of being an overseer and protector. This is not someone that is obsessive or controlling. This person has a genuine concern for your wellbeing and has your best interest at heart. They want to make sure you're not being hurt by anyone and that they're not hurting you either. That's what protection looks like.

In a dating context, if he drops you off, he makes sure that you get into the house safely. Or, if you're driving separately, calling you around the time that he thinks that you should be home to make sure you're okay. If you say, "Hey, I'm not feeling well today," he checks on you. A protector is going to be concerned whether your mind, spirit and soul are well. He makes sure that you are not mishandled or mistreated. This is something that I wrestled with. I never anticipated there to be an enemy within the camp. What I mean is it was not my expectation that the person that would hurt me the worst would be someone that I was closest to, most intimate with. My vulnerabilities and innermost things shared became part of the assault arsenal to try to break me. A man is supposed to not only protect you from the outside, but also be committed to protecting you within the walls of your home.

In addition to being a protector, love always trusts. Sometimes it's very difficult to trust a situation, and it can be challenging to trust people. But we are always able to trust God. Why? Because God is a man of His word. God has character. He does not change; He is consistent. God can be trusted, even if you're in a situation with your significant other and you don't know what the outcome is going to be. There might be an unexpected bill or medical diagnosis which surfaces. Maybe there is confusion in the relationship, and you're not sure what to believe. When you're not able to trust the outcome of the situation, you can wholeheartedly trust God. He never fails. Love protects. Love trusts. Love hopes.

Have you ever heard the term *negative Nancy*? With negative, Nancy something is always wrong and the glass is always half empty. This term is often used to describe a lady, but we know men can be negative too. Let's call him *negative Nelson*. Something will be found wrong even in perfection. Remember, negativity cannot operate in the realm of love. Love thinks the best. Love expects better days to come. "Honey we didn't have a good day today, but tomorrow will be better." "This was a bad financial season, the promotion didn't come through, but we are going to be okay." Love does not stay in a moment and allow that moment to define the rest of the story. Love hopes.

Love also perseveres. Have you ever had a season of people leaving your life - a parent who left physically, or one who is emotionally absent? Maybe you were married before, and one day your spouse announced they were leaving. They said they don't love you anymore. Or, perhaps an engagement ended unexpectedly. You thought your future would look a certain way based on the promises a person made, instead you've experienced rejection and a sense of abandonment. Despite what has happened in the past, a new love can change the narrative. Love is saying I am committed to walking this thing out with you. Even if it gets difficult, I'm still not going anywhere. This does not apply to abusive situations, because remember love is gentle, kind and not self-seeking. You are not tied to a situation which is harmful. Walking in love may be distancing yourself and praying for that person.

Now that we see all the qualities of love, at the very end of 1 Corinthians 13, it makes a closing statement. Faith, hope and love will always remain, and the greatest of these three is *love*. God highlights the importance of having His type of love. First, it's demonstrated by Him being in our lives. Secondly, we show God's love by having self-love. And thirdly, exuding the love God has given freely to us to others. The writer goes on to say when he was a child, he thought and acted like a child. But now that he is a man, he has to put away childish things. This sentiment highlights the importance of maturity.

Maturity is a quality of a good man. He is spiritually mature, mentally mature, and emotionally mature. It is one hundred percent possible to date someone who is an adult male, yet the conversations and emotional reactions feel elementary or adolescent. There's not a display of maturation within that individual. It can be very difficult when you're dealing with someone who physically looks like a grown man but acts like a child. And if you have children together, that's also very challenging. You want to show respect, but you're struggling not to parent him, particularly if his behavior is worse than the kids'. To avoid this, find a person who is mentally mature. He's worked through roadblocks and childhood trauma, so he is no longer like a toddler throwing a temper tantrum when something does not go his way.

I once was in a relationship having a conversation with my guy. One of the kids said something he didn't agree with. We talked about it. I communicated the other side of the story as rendered to me. I asked if we could move forward, and he said no because the kid was lying. In my mind, it was just a miscommunication. We talked about it, apologies were made and I thought the issue was resolved. However, later when it was the two of us alone, he told me that he couldn't believe that I didn't take his side. He then proceeds to throw himself on the floor and kick his feet and hands up and down on the ground, while insisting he was right. I kid you not. I literally watched a grown, 200 plus pound man throw a temper tantrum. Keep in mind, I don't even allow my children to throw temper tantrums. So, for me to watch a grown male kick and scream and throw a temper tantrum because his point of view was not received was mind blowing. This may seem very extreme, but I'm sure some of you have your own stories you could share similar to this.

A man with good character understands how to appropriately interact with another human being. He understands that he will not always get his way in life. And when he doesn't get his way, he knows it is not acceptable behavior to act out or become condescending. Having spiritual, mental, and emotional maturity is a must. I want to touch on the being spiritually mature side. We know that it is important for him to have a heart and love for Christ. However, he may be at a different place in his journey when you first meet. You may be more spiritually mature. I'm not referring to who has attended church longer. I'm referring to who has cultivated a personal relationship with God. It could be that you are more spiritually and emotionally mature. That's okay, as long as you are on equal footing surrounding your pursuit of faith. If he's a person who watches service online or doesn't have a church home, and you are a person who regularly attends service, serves and participates in small groups, there may be a misalignment. It's not a knock on him or his character, but the reality is that there may be a mismatch. You may not be equally yoked in this regard. Now if someone has recently given their life to the

Lord, you may be able to walk together in that journey, but it is important to not try to date somebody with the sole hope of leading them to Jesus. "If I can just get him to the altar, he will be a good man for me," "I know he's a babe in Christ, but when he grows up, he's going to be on point." No, this mindset doesn't work. Wait for him to mature. Time is a good thing. If he's for you, he's not going anywhere. Allow the time for development. God will let you know if this is your person and the right time and season for you to pursue or allow pursuit of a relationship.

As promised, I want to come back to the working quality. Earlier I alluded to the fact that a quality of a good man is that he works. I want to expound. A good man is going to have an occupation. It may be linked to his spiritual purpose, or it may not be. Either way, he is going to pursue work. When God made man, He gave him responsibilities, a job. This was before a woman even came into the equation. Hear me when I say a good man is going to have gainful employment.

This will look different for everyone. He may work a nine-to-five. He may work third shift hours. He may be an entrepreneur. He could be working on multiple things that allow him to provide for himself. He is not comfortable being in an environment where other people are taking care of him. He's not going to be still living at his mama's house or with family and not contributing financially. And if he so desires, he's working so that he can add a wife to his life. He's not okay with his woman providing EVERYTHING. If for some reason he finds himself in the season of unemployment, his full-time job is getting a new job. He is not lax about pursuing opportunities that will provide for him. God says a man that doesn't work doesn't eat, and a little folding of the hands and you'll have nothing. This man is about his business and does what's needed to cover his responsibilities. He's a visionary. And if he's not, he will connect with people who can help him go to the next level.

This is not an all-inclusive list of which qualities a good man should have, but it does serve as a building block of what to look for. The main thing he needs to have is the love of God in him. He could be a hard worker, diligent, a wonderful provider, very responsible, not childish, emotionally mature, but if he does not have the love of God in his heart, it is going to be challenging for him to overcome situations where you're not seeing eye to eye. If Christ is not the final arbitrator, who's going to decide how this thing should culminate. You have to choose to love him. He has to choose you. And when things get tough, the choice must be for you both to exude all of those qualities of love. There are many notable qualities, but the greatest of these is love ...God's kind of love.

Reflect

And in love he chose us before he laid the foundation of the universe! Because of his great love, he ordained us, so that we would be seen as holy in his eyes with an unstained innocence. Ephesians 1:4 TPT

Love is large and incredibly patient. Love is gentle and consistently kind to all. It refuses to be jealous when blessing comes to someone else. Love does not brag about one's achievements nor inflate its own importance. Love does not traffic in shame and disrespect, nor selfishly seek its own honor. Love is not easily irritated or quick to take offense. Love joyfully celebrates honesty and finds no delight in what is wrong. Love is a safe place of shelter, for it never stops believing the best for others. Love never takes failure as defeat, for it never gives up. I Corinthians 13:4 - 7 TPT

Finally, be strong in the Lord and in his mighty power.

Ephesians 6:10 NIV

Have I not commanded you? Be strong and courageous. Do not be afraid; do not be discouraged, for the Lord your God will be with you wherever you go." Joshua 1:9 NIV

Reflect

Don't hang out with angry people; don't keep company with hotheads. Bad temper is contagious— don't get infected.

Proverbs 22:24-25 MSG

Go ahead and be angry. You do well to be angry—but don't use your anger as fuel for revenge. And don't stay angry. Don't go to bed angry. Don't give the Devil that kind of foothold in your life.

Ephesians 4:26-27 MSG

"In prayer there is a connection between what God does and what you do. You can't get forgiveness from God, for instance, without also forgiving others. If you refuse to do your part, you cut yourself off from God's part. Matthew 6:14-15 MSG

Don't you remember the rule we had when we lived with you? "If you don't work, you don't eat." And now we're getting reports that a bunch of lazy good-for-nothings are taking advantage of you. This must not be tolerated. We command them to get to work immediately—no excuses, no arguments—and earn their own keep. Friends, don't slack off in doing your duty.

2 Thessalonians 3: 10 - 13 MSG

- 5 -

Introspect Check

Having a good man in your life is possible. The biggest part is simply identifying if he has the qualities of not only what you're looking for but also what you need. A relationship is not just one-sided, however. Having a great, intentional, loving, serving man who is so amazing and treats you like a queen is what you deserve. His presence makes you feel phenomenal, because he's just that kind of guy. But we need to look at ourselves to make sure we are showing up as *our* best selves. The single season is the opportune time for spiritual, mental, and emotional inventory. All of the qualities discussed in the previous chapter are things that need to be present and cultivated within us as well. If we don't have these qualities and if we are not expressing God's love, then we need to allow God to help us develop, before trying to partner with someone. There's a scripture in the Bible that talks about evaluation and addressing issues within yourself, before pointing them out and addressing them in someone else. It's important for us to do a deep dive and have some self-reflection, being willing to work on ourselves. So what exactly does self-love and work look like?

At the core of self-love is understanding who *is* love, which is God. We talked about this pertaining to the qualities of a good man. But I want to go a different route as it pertains to self-love. We have to know who we are as women in Christ. We are made in the image of God. We are His daughters, His masterpiece. The Bible says we are a royal priesthood, a chosen generation. You're not a mistake. You're not a mishap. No feature about you was a fluke. We are God's beautiful, wonderful, well-thought-out creation. He designed you just the way He wanted you.

Take a masterful painter, for example. They can paint one particular painting, which is absolutely beautiful and breathtaking, and then create another with different colors, texture and depth. It's beautiful like the first painting but in a different way. If it takes every day for you to look at yourself in the mirror and repeat *I am the Lord's masterpiece, I am wonderfully made, He's happy about me*, say it until you know it and believe it. God says He rejoices over us with songs. Basically, He's like, *yep that's mine. I made that. I'm so proud. I love her. She's so beautiful.*

It may take time if you've come up in a dynamic where you were not affirmed. Or, maybe you've been in relationships where someone told you that you weren't beautiful or that you were nothing. These are lies. And we have to allow what God says to transform the way we think. Anything that is contrary to what God says, even if it feels like truth, we have to understand that it's not. We must then work on getting our thoughts to align with our true identity. Read what God says, talk to God about what He says and surround yourself with other people who will affirm the things that God says about you. Eliminate the people, things and influences that are contrary. We are always being preached to. At all times of the day, there is a message seeking to influence you and move you to action. Either way, you're being fed something. If that vision is not, "Hey, I'm beautiful; I'm wonderful; I'm awesome", part of loving yourself is identifying and eliminating any voice contrary to that of God about who you are.

I love the process of self-discovery in Christ, because not only are you learning who He is, His nature and desires for your life, but you're also getting to see and experience new dimensions of who you are. You're the same person in the way that you look, the sound of your voice, but the inside has been transformed. You become a new person, a better person. You're not moving the same. You don't think the same. And if someone is not for your progression, keep it moving.

Embracing self-discovery is an important part of the journey. There are some traits that have been present for a very long time. At this junction, it's been accepted that this is who you are. For example, you may have a temper and will go off on people in a hot second. They had it coming, because they shouldn't have looked at you like that or made the comment. Evaluate the trait, thought and response in light of what God says. In the book of James God says that we should be slow to speak, quick to listen and slow to anger. This process of evaluation should be applied to any and everything. And a community of people will be able to help you with your blind spots.

In my culture, one of the things I was taught is that I shouldn't tell people my business. This taught me to put on a brave face when I left home that told the world everything was okay, and then deal with home problems in the privacy of home. I do believe everybody is not meant to be invited into your personal, sacred space. But a safe community needs to be established, one where you can share and grow with people you trust. The trust should be such that they can speak into your life honestly, and you can receive what they are saying, even if you don't agree with them. This doesn't mean they are right every time, but you make room to hear a different perspective.

Another part of self-love is healing and caring for yourself. For our physical being, we go to the doctor every year just to make sure your levels are good and that our bodies are okay. If we get sick, we take medication. If a bone is broken, it's reset or surgically mended. Time passes before pressure is applied again, or its being used in its normal cadence. Sometimes we do a better job taking care of ourselves physically, but a subpar job taking care of ourselves mentally, emotionally and spiritually. If you've been hurt relationally, the proper attention is needed to heal. Maybe you've gotten right back into another relationship, buried yourself in work or possibly acted like nothing happened. Like a storage closet, the wounds from a heartbreak, along with the bad memories, are stuffed way in the back. It's out of sight, out of mind, until something else happens and then you store that away too. But each time the hurt feels deeper or way too familiar. There may even be stuff in that closet from childhood. And when you open that closet, the culmination of stuffed emotions yields its narrative. "Nobody loves me." "I never get respect." "They always leave."

Words and phrases such as, *never, always, repeatedly, this happens all the time*, could indicate that there are some emotions and past experiences which need to be addressed. One day the closet is going to be opened, and I wouldn't want it to be the day where you meet the person that's actually really good for you. He's come into your life to love you, but then there's something that happens that reminds you of the past and all of that stuff comes falling out of the closet, because it's been stuffed and is pressing against the door of your heart. So, as soon as you open it up, everything comes rolling out, like an erupted volcano. And the person you're with now is buried underneath it all, along with you.

Even if you're not in a relationship when it finally all comes out, the same dynamic could occur from that door being opened by pressures at work, a financial crisis or physical sickness. You're faced with an overwhelming moment, because all of these things that have happened to you were not healed or processed through. From there, it's easy to get to a point where the walls really go up, and the thoughts pour in. "No, I'm not letting anybody come back into my heart. Don't come down the hall. Don't look at the door; it's locked." So many people have reached this point relationally, because they have been hurt time and time again. It's certainly a person's prerogative if they don't want to be in a relationship or to marry. Marriage is a gift but not a necessity. A person can have a very happy, successful and full life, not being in a relationship. Either way, the emotional hurts in that closet need to be cleared out. Healing has to occur, because you want to show up as your best self, for you and for those around you.

This process is not one you have to journey alone. You may need a counselor to partner with you along the way. All counselors are not the same. Finding a licensed, faith-based counselor is just one part. The other is finding one who's a fit for you. There needs to be a level of comfort, a relatable communication style and a rapport where trust can flourish. It may take a little time to find the right match, but don't get discouraged. Some counselors allow a 15-minute consultation to speak with them prior to scheduling a session. Talk to a couple of different counselors to get a sense of their personality and what they believe before moving forward. If you meet a counselor that doesn't really feel like a fit, try another.

For both men and women, counseling is such a powerful tool to help you walk through past hurts and traumas. For me coming up, it was taboo to get counseling and mental health was not an acceptable topic of discussion. I look at it this way, however. When we are young, we have coaches for everything. Whether T-ball, football, tap dance, cheerleading or you name it, there is a coach and system setup for skill development and success. We have all these different coaches throughout the early years of life, but for some reason, as soon as we get out of high school or college, coaching stops. The ironic thing is that the areas where we most need coaching, these are the areas we tend to stay away from. We need to make sure that we are whole mentally and emotionally, and not just at a particular point but throughout our lives. I encourage regular check-ins twice per year or once per quarter. Check-in and check-up. It can only help.

Counseling and coaching are wonderful tools in the process of being healthy and safe. However, the main component of wellness is cultivating a relationship with Holy Spirit. He is our counselor, God, and friend. This is as simple as talking to Him daily like you would your best friend. Or, if you haven't done it before, talk to Him like someone you just met. "Hey, this happened in my day and I feel this way about it. What do you think?" Look for scriptures surrounding that particular feeling. The neat thing is there are so many devotionals and interactive study experiences, which make it easy to plug into God. The more you do it, the more you learn to hear God's voice.

I have some really good friends, and if I heard a recording and couldn't see their faces, I would be able to pick out their voices, because I've spent time with them. I know how their voices sound. His voice may sound different to you than it does to the next person, but you'll know when He is speaking. I have a tone of voice that I use at work. I have a voice that I use on the phone. There's a different voice when I talk to my close friends. And even one with a slightly different tone when I speak with my children. Same person, but a different way of communicating in various scenarios. I choose the voice that will best reach who I'm communicating with. The same is true with God. He wants to speak uniquely and regularly with each of us.

Along with having a dynamic relationship with God, we all need a faith-based community to champion with us. When I got divorced, it was very difficult for me, because I felt as if I had lost everyone. I had to leave the church I had been a part of for about 14 years. Not only was I losing the access to extended family with whom I'd developed relationships, but I also lost my church community. I felt isolated and alone. I just know it was a God thing; He put me in a job at that time that wasn't the best, but I met a woman who invited me to her church one day when I shared I was looking for a small group. She actually extended an invitation to an upcoming women's conference. I remember thinking, "If I can just make it to Friday." I had battled so much emotionally, dealing with the divorce that I'd lost 20 to 25 lbs. within a month. I couldn't keep anything on my stomach, nor could I sleep well. It was a horrible season for me. But I continued to press into God with the energy and strength I had left. God says if you seek Him with all your heart, you'll find Him.

I didn't think I would make it, but God got me to that service. There was a song that I heard for the first time that night, *King of My Heart*. The lyrics resonated in my soul, reminding me that God is the king of my heart, and He is good. I don't remember all of what was said during the speaking time. But I do remember that song and I remember the lady who partnered with me in prayer. That night was the beginning of the shifting in my emotional climate. I've been at that church ever since that moment. I'm so grateful to be there, because everything that they do is with excellence. There are classes and courses on finances, dating, marriage, blended family. If there is an interest, there probably is a class or an opportunity for you to create a group for one. The focus is on cultivating disciples and helping people to become more like Christ, while fostering a community where people have fun and walk this life out the way God intended. Are there going to be challenges? Yes. Can you overcome them? Absolutely!

When you realize that you are down and running on empty, part of self-care is filling yourself up. Go to church. Surround yourself with people. Listening to your favorite online pastors is great, but there is purpose and power being in a brick-and-mortar building, where God can not only speak to you but also use your gifts to help someone else. I pray with people after service now, because there was someone there who prayed with me when I needed it most. I not only attend small groups, but I lead a small group that helps people get through difficult seasons. I do this, because someone helped me get through mine, so I know how life-changing it can be. It's not just about me getting through a moment or overcoming, it's about me helping others to do the same. God says the way we overcome is first through Jesus and also by sharing our experiences and how He got us through. Jesus had nails in his hands and feet, so I can show people my scars. The more we come together and the more we share, the stronger we become. It's not about a building. It just happens to be a place of worship and communion to help facilitate the spiritual and natural growth of God's people.

Being together also helps to develop accountability. God has given us all different gifts, some are to be pastors and teachers. If that were not needed, he wouldn't have said it. As the idiom goes, "Get in where you fit in." Find out where God wants you to plug in, and do it. Stay connected. Some of the closest relationships I have now are with people I've met in small groups. They have walked with me through challenging times and also been my plus one to dinner. Our kids hang out. We do life together. They know when I'm missing in action. They check on me, cover me, and help to keep me on track. This is what being part of God's family is about. It's like having built-in best friends. I tell my four children all the time that they will never be alone, because they are best friends. There's always someone to play with and talk to. God designed us to be with one another, and not just in a romantic way. We don't have to wait until we have a bae to do life with people. Whether you're married, in a relationship or single, we are designed for community.

Do you remember the cell phone special where your top five contacts could have unlimited calls and messaging? You weren't charged extra after a certain time to reach them. The slogan was, "Who's in your top five?" Well, who is in your five or ten or twelve? Jesus had a crew of twelve, and there were those who He was even closer to within the group. So if you don't have those relationships, start cultivating them. And it's okay if some relationships become closer than others. We see several instances where Peter and John went away with Jesus and it was just the three of them. It didn't mean He loved the other less, it was just the nature of that relationship during that season. Part of loving yourself and having self-care is fostering relationships with people who are safe, healthy and loving and who will be there to help pick us up when we fall and cheer us on when we win.

Someone once told me during a time when I was so excited about the progress I'd made, that they couldn't see it. I wasn't sad anymore after the divorce. I was active doing the things I loved to do. What did they mean they couldn't see it? I was finally in a celebratory season, but I guess this person didn't get the memo. Those words were very deflating. I was excited about what God was doing in my life, and they were holding me to a past I no longer lived in. I had to identify whose voice I was hearing. The truth was that even if the words were well intended, if they were not words of life or truth spoken in love, then that message wasn't for me. I don't care if it's a mother, father, a cousin or best friend from kindergarten, the people who are helping me grow the most are the ones who are in my top five, ten or twelve. If they are not adding value or fostering growth, then I reevaluate and pray about allowing them into my heart space. Everything in life comes from the heart. So, I have to make sure that the right stuff is going in and the right people are around. If the relationships in your life are not taking you to the next level, evaluate who is in your top five.

One of the other elements of self-care is addressing fear. When Adam and Eve sinned in the garden, they made clothes out of leaves and hid themselves because they were afraid. Sometimes people hide out of fear of something they've done or something that was done to them. And that fear is an inhibitor to stepping out boldly from the shadows, taking off the leaves and being completely exposed. One of the biggest fears that I had to work through was the fear of rejection and abandonment. There were several relationships where I felt that I showed up for others, but once the value I offered was added, those people left. I worked on facing these fears through doing things that I've shared with you. And although I have a background in the field of counseling, I have a counselor that I check-in with as needed. I read books related to self-development, listen to podcasts and read my Bible. And I love my small groups. All of these things have helped to transform not only how I see what has happened, but also how I respond to what is happening. Various traumas occurred, but my identity is not rooted in them. Addressing fear and renewing the mind allows you to wholeheartedly embrace all the things that God says and thinks about you.

What are some of the things that you're dealing with? What are you afraid of? What makes you sad? Do you find yourself being anxious? What upsets you? Spend time with God and ask Him to show you why you feel the way you do. If it's apathy, He will help you with that too, and show you various avenues to better deal with these feelings. Once resolved, you have a better understanding of who you are, the journey you've been on and ways to identify potential pitfalls.

A friend told me once that everybody has baggage, but make sure your bags are packed nicely. I can appreciate the sentiment of what she was trying to communicate. Everybody's got stuff they need to deal with, but make sure that when someone comes into your life, your stuff is not packaged as this hot, disorganized mess. They don't have a place to put their feet down, because *stuff* is everywhere. I would venture to take that statement a bit further and say, clean house as if you are relocating. The things that you take with you are those things that will benefit your future. God says to forget about the past, He is doing a new thing. If you go to a construction site, they cut down the trees, level the ground and build up from scratch. They don't take the rubble that was there before and start using the rubble in this brand new building. The rubble represents what was there before that has now been demolished. And that's what we do. We demolish the old way of thinking, and we clear the way for the new.

As you go through the process of introspection, remember what God says about you. You are not helpless. You are not unredeemable. Nothing that has happened to you is beyond the reach and stretch of God's hand on you. You are His precious daughter, His treasure. No matter what state you may be in right now, there's no place that God can't find you and bring you through. If you are alone, God sees you and wants to lovingly pull you close to Him. He will heal everything that hurts. And when you allow His hand into your heart, you are going to be a better version of yourself - Miss Lady 2.0. She's ready for one of God's sons in her life; she's not going to hurt him because of the hurts that still remain within her.

Reflect

Why would you focus on the flaw in someone else's life and fail to notice the glaring flaws of your own? How could you say to your friend, 'Let me show you where you're wrong,' when you're guilty of even more? You're being hypercritical and a hypocrite! First acknowledge and deal with your own 'blind spots,' and then you'll be capable of dealing with the 'blind spot' of your friend.

Matthew 7:3-5 TPT

But you are God's chosen treasure—priests who are kings, a spiritual "nation" set apart as God's devoted ones. He called you out of darkness to experience his marvelous light, and now he claims you as his very own. He did this so that you would broadcast his glorious wonders throughout the world.

I Peter 2:9 TPT

For the Lord your God is living among you. He is a mighty savior. He will take delight in you with gladness. With his love, he will calm all your fears. He will rejoice over you with joyful songs."

Zephaniah 3:17 NLT

Reflect

Don't copy the behavior and customs of this world, but let God transform you into a new person by changing the way you think. Then you will learn to know God's will for you, which is good and pleasing and perfect. Romans 12:2 NLT

Now, if anyone is enfolded into Christ, he has become an entirely new person. All that is related to the old order has vanished. Behold, everything is fresh and new.

2 Corinthians 5:17 TPT

As iron sharpens iron, so a friend sharpens a friend.

Proverbs 27:17 NLT

Wounds from a sincere friend are better than many kisses from an enemy. Proverbs 27:6 NLT

You will seek me and find me when you seek me with all your heart. Jeremiah 29:13 NIV

Reflect

"You don't get wormy apples off a healthy tree, nor good apples off a diseased tree. The health of the apple tells the health of the tree. You must begin with your own life-giving lives. It's who you are, not what you say and do, that counts. Your true being brims over into true words and deeds." Luke 6:45 MSG

They triumphed over him by the blood of the Lamb and by the word of their testimony;

they did not love their lives so much as to shrink from death. Revelation 12:11 NIV

"But forget all that— it is nothing compared to what I am going to do. Isaiah 43:18 NLT

- 6 -

Manage Your Expectations

A relationship is not a cure for loneliness. I know television shows would have you believe that a relationship may entail running through a field of knee-high grass and beautiful wildflowers. You can envision it. The sky is clear, kissed with a few clouds. The sun is beaming so beautifully bright. Yet there's not a drop of sweat beading from anyone's brow. There's a cool breeze gently tickling your skin as you gaze into each other's eyes. Never in this scene are there pesky insects or wind-tossed hair that is out of place. The semantic moment suggests that this is how a relationship should be when two people are deeply in love.

A beautiful moment such as this can be created, but it doesn't encompass the totality of what a relationship or marriage is like. Sometimes the idea of companionship is elevated to a point in our mind where we think that this is the panacea. We think a relationship or marriage will solve all of our problems. If you are a single mom, you may think *if only I had a partner to help me out a little bit, I would be happy*. So, maybe to you it's as simple as getting one night's rest when you feel like you're on the clock 24/7. Maybe you've been single for 5 to 10 years or more, and you just want to have someone to watch your favorite shows with, to go to see a movie with, to cook dinner in the kitchen and sit and enjoy a meal with. Maybe these are the gaps that a relationship will fill for you. Maybe you're somebody who likes to be on the go. You love traveling to distant places and making new experiences. A relationship would bring a partner with whom you can share stamps on your passports.

Yes, a partner or spouse absolutely can bring companionship, can travel with you, have dinners with you, or help out with the kids. They can be all of these things. However, it's so important that in the process you manage the image you have in your mind of what it should be versus the reality of what it will be. If there is an emotional void before entering into the relationship, the hole has to be filled *first*, in order to create a solid ground to build upon. If there are craters of needs and desires in a new relationship that have not been filled, as the foundation is laid and the general pressure of life is applied, that structure may experience a sinkhole effect. It's not because the building was defective; the collapse was due to a foundational issue. God tells us that we are to build our life upon Him. I'd venture that you've heard the saying that a single person needs to be complete and whole *before* entering a relationship. It has almost become cliché, something that's not always taken seriously. But it is serious, reason being that we often attract those things that we most desire. So even though we're attracting someone to fill space, it doesn't necessarily mean that the person is healthy. They fill the hole, but then as you start to build you realize the material is not up to code. This now puts you on the 10th floor of the building, and the ceiling is coming down. There are constant leaks from faulty plumbing. But if those holes are already filled, the person you're drawn to is more likely to pass inspection.

Another reason why it's so important to have those emotional holes filled is because it's going to better help you manage your expectations. Sometimes in relationships we can have unrealistic expectations of people. For example, if you have been single for a long time and you are expecting one hundred percent happy times with your new partner, that's not a realistic expectation. There should be more happy moments than sad, confusing or angry moments; but the truth is that it is not easy for two people who have lived individual lives with their own unique experiences up to this point to now bring their lives together. Space is shared. Finances are shared. Life is shared. So, each individual choice affects the unit collectively. What this means is there are still two ways of thinking, two vantage points. It is a process then for these two ways of doing things to become one.

Each person is learning and studying the other, so they can better understand how to show up best for their partner. What are the other person's likes? What disappoints them and makes them sad? Grasping the essence of another is an ongoing process that is not completed in year one, three, or even ten. There's always something to learn, because we are always changing. The human dynamic of relationships is intended to make us more like Christ. It is supposed to be a lying down of self in love and service of another. The expectation that has to be managed here is that your person is going to show up and immediately get everything about you. They will not disappoint you, and if you tell him one or two times, maybe ten, they're going to automatically be in tune with everything that you desire. He is a person. He's not perfect. And he needs grace, just as you and I do.

Another expectation that we have to manage surrounds children. These conversations are important to have in your courtship process or in premarital counseling. What are the expectations with children? How many kids do we want? Do we want children? If this is a blended family, what will the disciplinary roles look like? How will we manage the duality of routines and households? These are conversations that need to be had. Even with the best-made plans going into a blended family situation, there are other personalities that have to be considered and learned. It is going to be a process in getting to know new children, and if you have kids, for them to know your new boyfriend or husband as well. Allow Holy Spirit to guide you in best cultivating those relationships. This is not a microwave or approach. The goals should be learning, loving and respecting. Forcing children to immediately view someone new in their life as mom or dad can be tough for them. Give the relationships time to grow. Hopefully, prior to a couple coming together, there were healthy boundaries and discipline with the children. This way there is an atmosphere for respect and kindness towards the person they are being introduced to. Having a partner does not magically create a picturesque family. Expecting him to come in and immediately know how to best parent your kids is not realistic. Work together as a team, and be patient with one another.

Another critical set of expectations that I think has to be managed is regarding roles and ground rules. This one is easier to level set at the beginning of a relationship by simply having these conversations about what you think the roles should look like. Who's going to wash the dishes? Who takes out the trash? Which of you is better at handling the finances? Will you have two accounts or just one? Where and how are you going to spend holidays? Will both of you work? All of these things are expectations we may have internally, but they *have* to be communicated externally. Not only should they be vocalized, but listen, come into agreement and at some point verbally accept (with bold highlight, underline and exclamation marks) what the other person is communicating. The expectations on both sides should be crystal clear to each of you.

Oftentimes we get in relationships, and we don't say what we expect. We breeze over what we expect, thinking love will change the other person's mind. Or we hear what they say but completely dismiss it. Once we're married, we think it doesn't really matter. They will get over their issue. This way of thinking is a slippery slope. Open and honest communication about where you stand and how firmly planted you are on that expectation is the only way, if the relationship is something you both want to pursue. If you are a person that adamantly does not want children, say that. Don't give a person a glimmer of hope that once you get married, you'll consider having children when you know you don't want children *at all*. You need to communicate this vehemently. And once again, having those emotional holes filled before you enter into relationship won't allow you to go ahead and marry a man, thinking you'll just continue the conversation later down the road, when really the conversation has already transpired. The only thing needed was acknowledgement and acceptance on both sides of you guys not being on the same page on a very important issue. At some point prior to marriage, there needs to be mutual agreement as to the compromise that will be made or direction taken on the issue. An inability to reach this agreement should be a major red flag in moving forward.

The Bible says how can two walk together unless they agree. And this is so true; there has to be agreement in order to walk together peacefully. There literally needs to be a meeting of the minds early on in the dating process, before you become invested and there are emotions involved. Even with involving friends and family and allowing them to get to know each other, it makes it more difficult to step away once you discover that you are polar opposites on your "deal breakers".

I had a guy tell me after we had spent a lot of time getting to know each other and feelings were involved that he couldn't marry someone who drinks alcohol. I definitely respected his preference, but I was upset because he was aware when we met that I enjoy having a glass of red wine. This was something he felt very strongly about. My question to him was why didn't you tell me when we first met?

If there is something that is a deal breaker for you, communicate it up front. It gives the other person an opportunity to process the information, communicate their thoughts and make a decision on whether or not they want to adhere to your standard or walk away. Love allows choice. So these conversations are very important. What could happen if preferences and boundaries are not honored or discussed? Arguments can occur. One of you may not feel valued, or you may feel deceived, which impacts trust. Silence is not golden when it comes to expressing expectations. They must be communicated very clearly and both individuals need to be comfortable having healthy boundaries, where they can honor the other person as well as themselves.

Another topic to consider is finances. Financial difficulty is one of the leading causes of separation and divorce. Finances impact the economics of our society; it touches everything we do. We live in a world where you have to pay to live, to eat, and for transportation. Gone are the days of horses and buggies, houses built with your own hands and individual hunting and farming, for the most part. Money is just a part of daily transactions in life. So today there has to be an understanding of how money is going to be made and how much is needed to finance the lifestyle you both desire. I am not a proponent of marrying someone based on how much money is earned, because markets, interests and even the state of your health are subject to change. I believe character is the most important component. However, if there's an expectation surrounding a lifestyle you desire, maybe both people working or one person staying home, be forthright about it. Several people have said this to me over the course of time, and I love this statement. If you married a man today and he never changes the things that you are hoping he will, would you still commit to forever? What a sobering thought. Character and personality are things you definitely have to be able to live with, but you also have to evaluate the other areas that are important you. You are the one who has to live with the decision. If you're younger, this may be a little bit different, because the expectation is you're just starting the journey. But what is it the other person sees themselves doing? Is it something that will be a huge time commitment? Will it require extensive travel? What does your life together look like once the professional endeavors are brought into the equation?

The Holy Spirit has to be part of this journey, because we can have an idea in our minds that isn't necessarily God's best for us. For example, if one person has a desire to be a missionary and the other person wants to be a baker, what does that look like? Are you handing out muffins along the way? Possibly, but it's not as practical. There has to be an alignment in purpose and lifestyle. God has wonderful plans for us paired with purpose.

Even if nothing is "wrong" with a guy, and even if he has a super great personality and he is fun to be with, it's okay to walk away if God says, "Yeah that's my son. I love him and I love you, but there's somebody else I want you to meet. There is something I want you to do together, and you're going to be very happy." That requires faith. Everything that is brought to you is not necessarily for you. The next good person you encounter doesn't mean that person is your person. This expectation requires management. You may meet someone that's just going to be an amazing friend. Be open minded, and allow God to lead you. Your person and relationship may not look exactly how you think it will. But God can expand your vision and redirect you to something you never knew existed.

Another expectation that has to be managed is time. With all the conveniences in our society that technology brings, it causes us to have to work at being patient. The expectation is to have things right here, right now, ten seconds ago. When the answer is actually post dated. If you've been single for a while, divorced, or you've accumulated way too many bridesmaid dresses, you may start to grapple with comparison and wonder why them and not you. No one person is better than the next; however, we all have our own life stories. The best thing we can do while on the journey is focus on becoming. Every day improves upon the next. And walking with Holy Spirit is so much fun. Let me tell you, if you don't have a tight relationship yet you're really missing out because He is so funny and personable. He genuinely is the best friend in the entire universe. There's nothing you can't talk to Him about from what you're going to wear that day to who upset you. He is amazing at filling your heart's desire for companionship. He definitely acknowledges the need and longing for human companionship, because when God made us, He was the one who said it was not good for us to be alone. If you have ever felt bad about feeling alone, that's okay. It's totally real and acceptable. Even in the presence of God, there is still a need for human interaction. That's why He made more people. So when you find yourself in a lonely space, spend time with God first, and then get out and spend time with people. Even if you are not in a relationship with a man, it's so imperative to be in relationship with healthy people.

The timing of you meeting someone, developing a friendship, and eventually entering into a relationship or marriage looks different for everyone. But one thing I love about God is that He redeems time. When He moves, things move very quickly and concretely. His Word does not return to Him void and always accomplishes what He sets it out to do. This is something you can rest your hat on. Singleness is not a curse or punishment; it is a state of being. It just may be you right now or you and the kids, but that doesn't stop the fun. Live life, and live on purpose. Enjoy the right here, right now.

I was talking to my daughter a few weeks back about what I was going to do while on vacation. The kids will be away for a few weeks during the summer and I want to do something fun. So, my daughter proceeds to tell me, "Mom you should have a hot girl summer." I paused for a second, because I had not heard of this term before. I said, "Honey, what's a hot girl summer?" When I was coming up it had a meaning that I was sure she wasn't referring to, so I wanted more details on what she was trying to communicate. She then proceeds to ask Siri for the definition of a hot girl summer. Siri does her thing and pulls up the results. My daughter reads me the definition. And it's basically looking your best, feeling your best, going out, enjoying yourself, having a good time, feeling beautiful and confident. I said, "Okay! I can do that. I can go and have a hot girl summer." Why don't we apply that to this season of singleness? Why don't we have a hot girl single season, where we are feeling good, looking good, participating in self-care and doing those things that makes us smile. No pressing pause or punting them down the field waiting for someone to show up before we go travel, buy a house or move to the area where we desire to live. Those things are great to do with someone, but you don't have to wait; you can do those things now. I encourage you to. Have a hot girl single season. Live your best life, while walking with Holy Spirit.

Any thought that suggests a relationship with God is limiting couldn't be farther from the truth. Miscommunication and bad examples have helped to perpetuate that impression. However, God said he came to give us life and one that is full. As a father, He wants nothing more than for His children to do well and be well in body and in soul. That's truth. You are a daughter of the King, His princess. He says if we can give our children good things, how much would He give us as His children. Understanding this truth helps in those moments when you may question God about where your mate is. When time doesn't seem to be your friend, God is. And He has something, someone good for you.

People don't necessarily make the situation feel better. Has anyone asked you, "Why aren't you married?" "Why haven't you had kids yet?" "Why are you out so much? You should be home so you can meet somebody." Don't allow somebody to project their limitations and thoughts on you. You have your own life to live, and as long as you're walking with Holy Spirit, then live that life. Jesus was on the beach with Peter after He'd been crucified and was resurrected. During that conversation, He was talking to Peter about his mission of building the church and forewarning that at some point he would die. Peter sees John in the distance and was like, "Lord, what about him?" Jesus' response was don't worry about him. I'm talking about you. And that's how we have to be...at a place where we are not comparing ourselves to someone in the distance. "I thought I would be married by 28." "I wanted to have children by 35." Whatever the mental milestone is, replace it with, "I believe I will see the goodness of the Lord in the land of the living," according to God's promise.

God works from an infinite platform, while we work in a finite reality. So the timing and details of what various milestones look like should be erased or at least become fluid. The boxes that are missing check marks may be partly attributed to feelings of sadness and unfulfillment, because things have not happened in a given timeframe. But who set the clock and made the checklist? Bringing your expectations to God will level set your life. And while you hold to your hope, live and enjoy. Wake up on a Saturday morning, put on your favorite music. Dance around the house in your cami and undies. Go outside on your patio and drink something refreshing. Look at the beauty of nature, hear the birds chirp and feel the heat from the sun beam on your face. Throw your hair back and wave it in the wind. Have a hot girl single season! And then when someone does show up, they can join the party and experience the joys of your life with you. Their presence will be an addition to your fullness, because you're not waiting on anyone to *be* the moment, you are living the moment and inviting them into that space.

Reflect

Can two people walk together without agreeing on the direction? Amos 3:3 NLT

As the rain and the snow come down from heaven, and do not return to it without watering the earth and making it bud and flourish, so that it yields seed for the sower and bread for the eater, so is my word that goes out from my mouth: It will not return to me empty, but will accomplish what I desire and achieve the purpose for which I sent it. You will go out in joy and be led forth in peace; the mountains and hills will burst into song before you, and all the trees of the field will clap their hands.

Isaiah 55:10-12 NIV

A thief has only one thing in mind—he wants to steal, slaughter, and destroy. But I have come to *give you everything in abundance, more than you expect*—life in its fullness until you overflow!

John 10: 10 TPT

Beloved, I pray that you may prosper in all things and be in health, just as your soul prospers.

3 John 1:2 NKJV

Reflect

If you, imperfect as you are, know how to lovingly take care of your children and give them what's best, how much more ready is your heavenly Father to give wonderful gifts to those who ask him?"

Matthew 7:11 TPT

I'm sure now I'll see God's goodness in the exuberant earth. Stay with GOD! Take heart. Don't quit. I'll say it again: Stay with GOD.

Psalms 27:13-14 MSG

- 7 -

Options

Should I expect or hold out for another? This is a question many ponder particularly with the societal concept of keeping your options open. I know when I go shopping I do my research, especially when it comes to making a large purchase. So if I'm looking for a home, I will consider 4 to 5 lenders that may fit my criteria. The same goes for cars. I'm going to evaluate the seating capacity, safety features, bells and whistles, and I'm definitely going to need a test drive. This approach is great when it comes to goods and services. However, the consumer mentality required for the marketplace doesn't fair as well when applied to relationships. We are not to consume people; we are to enjoy them. And yes, there is place to evaluate character, morals, personality and common ground, but this is different than viewing people as disposable or treating others as commodities. The relational human dynamic should be one of appreciation, valuing the uniqueness in others. In the process of dating and getting to know someone, it's important to remember there is a person on the other side of the exchange. It's not transactional, like a blouse you decided at the register to go back and trade for another. There is no replacement for people. Even if you come to discover that a person isn't your guy, how you handle him still matters. It takes a little trust to let go of wanting to select every single feature. Your guy may not fit exactly in the box, but he will be the right fit for you.

I'm learning to appreciate this area of gray in not knowing the details about who my man will be. I do believe some of the desires I have will be represented in my person, as far as his character. And I don't think he'll be unattractive to me by any means. But the other details like his job and hobbies are in the gray. I'm okay with that, because I've come to realize that I have to be in a place of complete surrender. Goodness knows I've done it my own way a couple of times before. I picked the guy with the looks. I picked the guy with swag. I picked one that looked good on paper. I picked all of those things, and it did not serve me well. As my relationship has grown with God, I better understand His character. I know He is good and He loves me. So He can show me things and let me know what and who is going to be good for me. I can trust Him.

Say, for instance, a person is a marine biologist. Great profession, but it's not something on my current radar. I could be swimming with dolphins and laced in scuba gear one day, and I'm open to it. I'm open to moving along with Holy Spirit. Because even if the package doesn't look exactly the way I thought, but I feel the impression upon my spirit to pursue, I'm not going to be over here thinking, "Okay, well I'm just going to continue to keep these other options open." If God is letting me know this is my person, why would I jeopardize that? It reminds me of the passage where John the Baptist asked, Lord, *are you the Messiah or should we expect another?* Legit question, since at the moment he was having some doubts. Jesus affirmed him that indeed He was the one. So, John stood on that affirmation in boldness and faith, when he could have chosen to still doubt and look.

I don't ever want to miss my opportunity, because I'm in a consumerism mode, thinking there's going to be something better and looking for the next, hedging my bet. Gambling doesn't guarantee a win, and if I do win, that same mentality which got me there will cause me to lose more than I ever gained. I would hate to have gone through seasons of preparation, growth and development to get the healthy relationship I've been praying for, only to squander or bypass it because it doesn't look exactly the way I expected it to look. If I'm keeping my eyes open for someone who checks all the external boxes and not the internal ones, I may miss the person who's going to treat me like his treasure.

Now in the same light of being able to move forward when God says to move, there must also be a willingness to walk away when He shows you that it's not right. Some of the options are actually distractions and need to be eliminated. We can overcomplicate the decision-making process with logic and reasoning. To this I will say, let's go back to the basics. I've heard people say everything you need to know in life you learn in kindergarten. Be kind to others. If you don't have anything nice to say, don't say anything at all. Choose the best answer. One plus one equals two. The people that come into your life should not cause you to question or challenge the basic principles. When you're taking a test, you choose the best option even if you didn't know the exact answer. Some of them could be eliminated because they just don't make sense. So when God says to not be unequally yoked, this standard is applied to the options. If you meet someone and they are practicing some other religion, that doesn't mean that you can't be friends, but being in a relationship is not an option. A date to save approach isn't wise. Disrespect is another eliminating factor. If someone is speaking to you disrespectfully, that's an absolute no and this option needs to be eliminated. It doesn't matter if he is having a difficult time right now, or it comes from how he grew up. The reason behind it is between him and Jesus. Disrespect is absolutely unacceptable.

Sometimes there doesn't have to be a specific reason for you to remove yourself from an equation. If that gut feeling or women's intuition felt deep down in the pit of your stomach is telling you that something is not right, then that is enough. You may not be able to put your finger on it and understand the feeling, because *nothing* is wrong. But something *is* wrong. This is when we have to trust Holy Spirit and resist the urge to fast forward through that internal pause. If you are developing an ear for God's voice, that gut check is God warning you, so trust it. And know that time is not your enemy. Time is actually your friend. You get to observe and see how they react and relate to others, how they handle stressful situations and what comes out of their mouth when no one is really watching. The more time spent observing provides greater clarity on who they really are. So don't be in a rush.

If you've been single for some time or want to start a family by a certain age, this can apply pressure to the decision-making process. But here is something that may bring some relief. It is very true that time is passing. Every year we do get older. But is making the wrong choice about who to be with worth having a family with someone who isn't the person you initially thought them to be? As time passes, you are able to glean their true character, which is not conducive to the dream you envisioned of a husband, father, and provider. And now you're having to shield the kids from seeing and hearing certain things that aren't healthy. On top of that, you have to pretend to be happy. That's not living your best life and doesn't compare to your hot girl single season of joy, peace and freedom.

It's okay to take your time. The one who is for you is not going anywhere, and God will confirm that in your heart and your spirit. Enjoy the warm, fuzzy, ice cream and butterfly feelings. But give a relationship time for those butterflies to fly and for the ice cream to melt, so you can see what's left. Because after those feelings wane a bit, there will stand the person that you have to choose to love every single day, because love is a choice. If that person is toxic, abusive, or just doesn't treat you right, that's not something that's meant to be sustained. Understand when to hold them and when to fold them. Some options just need to be eliminated, others need to be evaluated, and then there is the *one* which will be celebrated. All the heavens will celebrate along with you, and that's worth waiting for.

Reflect

Within your heart you can make plans for your future, but the Lord chooses the steps you take to get there.

Proverbs 16:9 TPT

-8-

Love Me to Tears

We talked about managing expectations. One of the beautiful sides of facing reality, level setting, and understanding what God says about your heart's desires is also honoring what you *do want* in a man. In my experiences of love and relationships, there have been a lot of tears. There have been tears of sadness, regret, hope deferred and longing for better. This chapter is entitled "Love Me to Tears", because this time I want to be loved so deeply that my tears are happy. My tears will say, "I can't believe you're this amazing. Wow, look how good God is to me. Jesus, did you really just redeem the time? God you are faithful!" Yes, I still want the tears, but this time they'll be tears of gladness.

Repeatedly in the book of Psalms, we see the directive

for people be filled with joy, laughter and dancing. There is an acknowledgment of difficulty and trials, but through these seasons and certainly after they have passed, there is a heart of expectation and joy. God not only cares about the environments around us but also the desires within. He says to delight yourself in Him, and He will he give you your heart's desires. What are the unspoken things you desire in a mate? What is it that you don't say out loud, just in case it doesn't happen and you don't want to be disappointed?

I took a class with maybe twenty other ladies; it was led by a phenomenal woman. She was a wife and a mother who had a passion to help women and new couples understand what this marriage thing looks like, how to prepare for it and how to navigate the challenges. One of the things that we had to do for an exercise was to write down the top ten things that we desire in a person. Before that exercise, I had not spent the time thinking through what I desire overall. What does the entire package look like for me? There was space to write down ten things I wanted and ten absolute no go's or deal breakers. It was transformational to be able to see on paper what it is that I really want in a person, alongside the things that I didn't. I'm going to share a few of my deep desires. And I want you to start thinking through yours, and writing them down, if you haven't done so already.

So, for me the number one thing is that he has an intimate relationship with Jesus. If he doesn't have the wherewithal to take direction from Christ, submit to His authority and be led by the Spirit, he won't be able to love me or lead me well. God is the one who teaches us how to love. Even if a man has a great personality, when the rubber meets the road and difficult times happen, what's going to come out? I had someone put it this way, "You always know what's inside a person by what comes out when they are squeezed." In times of change or angst, does he start cussing and fussing and being disrespectful or does he reflect, pray, and communicate? Whatever is inside is what's going to come out during difficulty. I want Jesus to be inside that person, so what comes out is forgiveness, compassion, courage, patience, and stick-to-itiveness. He needs to have an intimate relationship with God, because if he understands God's love for him, he can best love me.

We talked about the qualities of a good man, the importance of having the fruit of the Spirit. And those qualities are evident in how he treats me, the children, those around him, and how he carries himself in life. One of the things that I love most is when I go into a restaurant and I can smell the food cooking from the outside. It draws me in, because of how wonderful it smells. I can almost taste the food before I'm even seated at the table because of the aroma. That is the experience I want to have with a man. The sweet aroma of the Holy Spirit leaves an impression when he's in the room. I know that God is there, because I can see the fruit of His presence.

As a wife and as a partner, I want to come alongside my man and help to be his level up. Whatever God-given vision he has, I want to help him fulfill it. But he has to have a vision. The details may be fuzzy, but the outline must be there. Otherwise, the relationship is subject to come to a fork in the road, where I'm going after one thing and he is going after another. But if there is a roadmap before I come on board, I can better determine if this trip is one that I'm supposed to take. If he knows what God has assigned him to do, then he can identify if I am a good partner for him as I'm doing the same. And if it's a yes, we can be dynamic and walk this thing out together.

Funny. Hilarious. Comical. I want him to have a great sense of humor. Talk about loving me to tears, I want to laugh until my belly aches and my eyes water. What it would be to have that dynamic, where we can talk about anything and laugh about everything. Just because we love Jesus, it doesn't mean every punch line is a scripture and each conversation feels like a Bible study. We can actually make fun of each other in a very kind, loving and playful way. God says that laughter does well like medicine. So, having a sense of humor is huge for me.

I've experienced two extremes surrounding humor. One guy, who was an absolute sweetheart, didn't get most of my jokes or many things I tried to communicate for that matter. He would often ask, "What do you mean?" It was like a deer in headlights. He just didn't get it. Although very intelligent, we just weren't on the same page. Then on the other end of the spectrum, there's the guy who only laughs at his own jokes or if he's low key picking at me. And one of my mantras is that it's not funny, unless both people are laughing; laughter isn't to be used as a weapon.

Timing also matters. If there is a serious moment, then a person needs to be able to pivot in that space. But the core of him is joy, which exudes from his pores effortlessly. I get him and he gets me, and we are able to incorporate humor at the heart of our relationship.

Along with us having a sense of humor, I also want to enjoy the company of others. I enjoy being with friends, sharing a meal, making moments and memories. Though I love a good vacation, I don't want to be ostracized on an island. In past relationships, I've experienced this. I didn't have a community outside of that individual. Literally, it was just me and that person, and a lot of times we didn't do the things that made me happy or brought me joy. So in the next season, I want my man. I want my village. And I want to have fun.

In all things, balance is important. So along with being super funny, I also want him to have a serious side in respect to being able to protect me and provide for me. That's not just in a financial sense. His presence is power. Can he show up when there's a need and solicit whatever resources are required in a given situation? Does he perceive danger and navigate away from it, or does he attract it? Being physically, emotionally, and spiritually safe is paramount. Part of caring and expressing love is covering me and having my back. He sees the landscape from a different vantage point and shines light on things that I may not see. He perceives needs before being asked.

It takes selflessness to love extravagantly. God demonstrates His love for us by literally laying down His life. And that's what He asks of a man who marries one of His daughters, for that man to lay down his life for his wife. Individual preferences are no longer the priority. Serving your partner and loving them well becomes the badge of honor. The way he handles me is unmatched. This has become my expectation, because it's God's desire for His daughters.

It's one thing to start, but it's another to finish and finish well. Commitment is important. And commitment means loving like Christ loves the church. We see how Jesus laid his life down for those he loves and this is the example God asks men to follow pertaining to their wives. The way he loves should point me to Jesus. I shouldn't have to ask God, "Is this your son? Did you really make this creation? I know you said it wasn't good for me to be alone, but right now I'd rather be alone than deal with this foolishness." No, his presence isn't going to elicit feelings of doubt, insecurity, questioning God and wondering why I'm being treated in a less than favorable way.

Proverbs 31 says a woman who honors God should be praised. It asks where can you find a woman of value, a woman of virtue? She is worth more than rubies. She is a treasure. She is a crown to her husband. And a crown is symbolic of honor, leadership, and authority. Her presence makes a statement even from afar. When you see a king with a crown, it's apparent that he has authority and power. A good woman in his life signifies that. He in turn honors her. Not as a trophy, but as an indispensable part of his leadership.

The last three "must haves" that I wrote down during the exercise was that he must be great with children, since I have four wonderful treasures. I want someone who is going to love and protect my children, because they are part of me. God brings husbands and wives together to have and to raise Godly children. And although they will not be his biological children, he will be instrumental in displaying Christ to them. And vice versa, if he has children. The idea is to model what love looks like, so they can grow and go into the world and love well. I'd also like for him to be romantic. It doesn't take much to make a moment magical. A little listening, coupled with observation and action, is the recipe of romance. Life is not a movie, but it is what you make it! So, I want us to show up for each other in unique ways. Last but not least, I want there to be some type of physical attraction. I'm open to heights, shades, and shapes but I need to be able to kiss him with my eyes open. If I had to give a sketch artist a description of what he may look like, I could do it, but I'm open minded as well. I'm not going to attempt to put God in a box in this area. God knows what I need and what I like, and He will pull it together in such a way that pleases my heart.

Are your wheels turning yet regarding your own must haves? What does God say about the things you've identified? Pray about it, and see if there is anything on the list that precludes the person that He has for you. God sees. He hears, and He cares. So take some time to write those things down, so you are cognizant of what you are looking for. When you know what your heart desires, you won't waste time compromising with yourself as it relates to something you *know* is needed in your relationship.

Intuitively, your list of *must not* have qualities in a mate would be the exact opposite of all of the qualities that you just listed. I would encourage you to go a little deeper when you're writing this list. Try to think of other things outside of the exact opposite of what you said you wanted. For example, for me someone who lies, cheats, is mean, has questionable character, married or in a relationship, has not healed from a past relationship, is selfish or narcissistic, has no friends or accountability and someone who's controlled by money are *must not* have qualities. These are different from the must have qualities, which should be polar opposites. Nonetheless, having an understanding of what you don't desire will help in navigating the dating space.

The opposites of the qualities desired are gauges as well. I want someone who loves children. Therefore if he doesn't like kids, that's obviously not going to work. He needs to have a real relationship with God. Therefore, someone who has a superficial relationship and puts on a church face is a no go. Whatever your *must not* have qualities are, write them down. That way you can hold yourself accountable and not compromise on these things because you're lonely or ready to start a family. It never fails that once you've cleaned house and gotten rid of old habits and developed healthy boundaries, the hater of your soul is going to come back stronger and he may even present a counterfeit person to detour you. When you're confident, feeling good about yourself, have biblical community, focused on your goals, and your walk with God is on point, be on the lookout for distractions. And these distractions may just come from your *must not* have list.

The enemy does not want you advancing or partnering with a man who is after God's heart. The two of you together is a powerful threat to the kingdom of darkness. So, you'd best believe he is going to send a counterfeit who may look like he has a few nice qualities, just to gain proximity to you. The man could be fine, economically stable and looks like he has it together. This is where the must-haves and must not haves come into play. It's going to help you look at a spectrum of qualities and not just the ones that are initially presented. Let's face it, it's exciting when you meet someone and have chemistry. But the aim is to enjoy the moments but not get swept away in them, certainly without due diligence. Your boundary lists are going to help you stay true to those things you desire and have prayed over.

God loves you, and you are special to Him. He cares about what you care about. You are not lost or forgotten. He captures every tear and intimately knows your heart's cry. He is faithful and will bring someone into your life who's going to love you just the way He has designed and intended for you to be loved. The love to be experienced is not fake, cheap or temporary. It's not going to be something that you have to share romantically with someone else. It is going to be yours and yours alone, because it's to emulate God's love. Your husband is out there, and he is going to love all parts of you, from your appearance to your heart to your laugh. He is going to love you, exclusively.

When I was coming up, there was a commercial for a baby shampoo. In the commercial, it displayed a baby taking a bath, laughing and splashing in the tub. When the soapy water got on the baby's face, it didn't bother the child at all. The narrator commented that the shampoo was gentle on the eyes, and there are no more tears. I believe that God has someone for you that's going to be gentle with your heart and there are not going to be any more tears. There's a scripture that says God will give you a garment of praise, instead of a heavy spirit of despair. Going forward your life will be one of gladness, and if there are tears, they will be tears of joy.

Reflect

Take delight in the LORD, and he will give you the desires of your heart. Psalms 37:4 NIV

A cheerful heart is good medicine, but a broken spirit saps a person's strength. Proverbs 17:22 NLT

and provide for those who grieve in Zion—

to bestow on them a crown of beauty instead of ashes, the oil of joy instead of mourning, and a garment of praise instead of a spirit of despair. They will be called oaks of righteousness, a planting of the LORD for the display of his splendor.

Isaiah 61:3 NIV

Lord, you know everything there is to know about me. You perceive every movement of my heart and soul, and you understand my every thought before it even enters my mind. You are so intimately aware of me, Lord. You read my heart like an open book and you know all the words I'm about to speak before I even start a sentence! You know every step I will take before my journey even begins.

Psalms 139:1-4 TPT

Reflect

Wives, understand and support your husbands in ways that show your support for Christ. The husband provides leadership to his wife the way Christ does to his church, not by domineering but by cherishing. So, just as the church submits to Christ as he exercises such leadership, wives should likewise submit to their husbands.

Husbands, go all out in your love for your wives, exactly as Christ did for the church—a love marked by giving, not getting. Christ's love makes the church whole. His words evoke her beauty. Everything He does and says is designed to bring the best out of her, dressing her in dazzling white silk, radiant with holiness. And that is how husbands ought to love their wives. They're really doing themselves a favor—since they're already "one" in marriage.

No one abuses his own body, does he? No, he feeds and pampers it. That's how Christ treats us, the church, since we are part of His body. And this is why a man leaves father and mother and cherishes his wife. No longer two, they become "one flesh." This is a huge mystery, and I don't pretend to understand it all. What is clearest to me is the way Christ treats the church. And this provides a good picture of how each husband is to treat his wife, loving himself in loving her, and how each wife is to honor her husband.

Ephesians 5:22-33 MSG

Reflect

Charm is deceptive, and beauty does not last; but a woman who fears the LORD will be greatly praised. Reward her for all she has done. Let her deeds publicly declare her praise.

Proverbs 31:30-31 NLT

- 9 -

Throw Yourself a Party

Celebrate yourself. It took me a long time to really get to the point where I was okay and intentional about taking care of myself. So many times I would set goals, check them off and then move on to the next thing. In the process of doing life, getting married and having children, I put everybody else first. Having a heart to serve others is important, since that is what we are supposed to do. Yet, we are also to love ourselves. God says to love Him with everything and then to love our neighbor as ourselves. This means the standard of loving your neighbor stems from loving yourself. If you are kind, patient, forgiving, and caring towards others, you have to extend the same grace to yourself.

Let's focus on celebrating the wonderful diamond,

treasure and queen that you are. You are resilient, absolutely phenomenal. You're still pressing forward and you've made it to this point. With everything you've gone through, each setback, disappointment, challenge, promotion, or victory, you're still here. You didn't give up. You didn't quit. I'm proud of you and you should be proud of you too!

It's important to continually assess where you are. Are you on the go, burning the midnight oil, trying to exceed expectations and please everyone? I want you to take a pause and celebrate yourself. In the middle of your checklist, at the end of each day, stop and acknowledge that you did great today. Say it out loud. "Hey, you know what... I did a great job at closing out that report today." "Hey, I did a great job getting dinner ready and getting these kids in the bath." Yes you may do the same tasks every day, so it doesn't seem like much of an accomplishment. But you did it while you were tired. You pushed through when you were sick. You served others when you needed a helping hand. You were drained mentally and emotionally, yet you still showed up. Tell yourself, "Good job!" Life and death are in words. Even if you are that person that affirms everyone else, you need to speak life over yourself as well.

There's an app that sends affirmations throughout the day. Every two hours or so it will tell me things like, "You are worthy of love." "Your future is great." "Wonderful things are coming." When I receive the notification, I say the affirmation aloud, because it affirms the things I already know about

myself or fuels my fire and gives me vision of the woman that I am becoming. It produces hope, which is a state God wants us to live in. Even if you're in a place where you don't feel that you've accomplished much, have had several setbacks or don't feel worthy, there is still something to celebrate. Do you know why? It's because what you have been through does not define you or give you value. Your value comes from God and the price He paid for you was His life. Even at your lowest point, you are still praise worthy. God himself rejoices over you. So tell yourself good things every day. Not once in a blue moon, but every single day.

When you start to work on your self-esteem and value, your identity becomes more solidified. And over time your self-love tank becomes full. Then when someone gives you a compliment, you can accept it without question or necessity. Sometimes in dating it's easy to get caught up in someone's words, if you are not used to hearing compliments or find yourself needing them. The words produce a feel good sensation. And if you're not careful, those words can be a distraction to red flags. However, when *you* celebrate the great woman you are, anything you receive outside of that is just a bonus.

Get an affirmations app or make a digital playlist. Look at yourself in the mirror and say something positive. Your mind is going to speak to you throughout the day anyway, so train it to be kind. Give it the words that you want to think about and meditate on to uplift yourself. Someone once asked me what are the things I say to myself in my head. They asked if the things I say to myself, I would also say to my daughter or best friend. Would I say them to my three-year-old self? If the answer is *no* to any of these questions, then the narrative in your mind needs to be shut down and reframed. Frankly, you need to start a brand-new conversation.

If you don't like where you are, start speaking to where you want to be. You are beautiful. You are intelligent. You are entrepreneurial. You can get the promotion. Whatever the desire, if your mind or others have placed limitations on you, it's time to break free from limiting thinking. God has a plan for your life. He says it's good and full of hope. You may know the famous scripture found in Jeremiah 29:11, which speaks of God knowing the *good* plan He has for you. But right before that verse, God sent His people into an unfamiliar place. But even in that space, God told them to progress forward, to build, and to *grow*. He tells them to not dwindle away but to pray for where they are and know that something greater is ahead. So the narrative upstairs needs to be positive, full of hope and grounded on God's presence and willingness to do great things in your life. God's image is on you. His Spirit lives in you. This is something to celebrate.

Another aspect of self-love is doing things that you enjoy. I've been in relationships where I was isolated and not really allowed to express myself. Over time I became sad, because I wasn't free to be me. A relationship should add to who you are, not subtract from your being. I want you to feel comfortable and confident in being who God made you to be. He gave you interests and passions, an entire world to explore. If He doesn't have a problem with it, nor should anyone else. God smiles when you smile, so if you don't know, try things until you figure out what you enjoy. Reflect on the last time you did something fun, then go and do that. If it's hiking, then go for a hike. Do you like to journal, fish, knit, play basketball, see a play? Whatever the activity that invigorates you or brings you peace, do it!

Just because you're single, doesn't mean you can't have fun. The party is now, because life is happening now. And tomorrow is not promised. Be your best self now. Celebrate now. Have that hot girl summer now! That's all part of loving and being kind to yourself.

If you haven't carved out time for yourself in a long time, start with one or two activities a month. Order a planner, and use your phone or digital calendar to mark off time that is exclusively for you. The next month add something else. Plan ahead; purchase the tickets; make the reservations. Invite a girlfriend to dinner or have a movie night. If you have kids and your friend does as well, then invite everyone over and have a party with card games, dance offs and snacks. Just start intentionally incorporating fun, little by little. It definitely shifts the focus from what or who you don't have in your life back to the wonderful things and people that you do have. I have a planner full of activities for myself and for family time with the kiddos. This means the pockets of loneliness are few and far between. I started this shortly after my first divorce, because I found that when the children were away for the weekend or during holiday breaks, I would feel the emptiness in the home. But once I started moving and doing, I felt great! There are so many outlets and interest groups where you can connect with people who like to do the same things as you. And if you have kids, there are women in the same boat who find activities that incorporate the entire family. There is nothing to limit you or hold you back. So go for it!

Another part of celebrating yourself is cultivating your gifts. We are fashioned after God, yet individually wired. Just as there is Father, Son, and Holy Spirit, which are all God, they all have different roles. We too have different characteristics, natural bents and personalities. Sometimes we can get caught up in comparison, maybe wanting accolades of another or approval, which can lead to seeking activities or careers that would put us in the spotlight. It's essential to understand we are part of the body; *part* being the essential word here. There are many parts of the Body of Christ, but an eye can't be a toe and an ear can't be a foot. All the parts are needed to function as a whole, as it was designed. When we are confident in whom God made us to be, quirks and all, then that's when we function well, our best. Not only are we the best for ourselves, but we also function in a capacity that positively impacts the entire body.

I know a lady, and she is one of the funniest people that I have personally encountered. Practically everything that comes out her mouth is hilarious. However, sometimes she will draw back and get quiet. From what I gather, it is from fear of being rejected or from someone laughing *at* her, not *with* her. However, humor is part of her giftedness. Her presence brings joy and happiness. Never in a million years did I think she is too silly or over the top. She is amazingly witty, jovial and awesome. The way she thinks on her feet and lights up a room can bring tears to your eyes from laughter. I don't know if she fully sees just how much of a joy she is to others, but I *see* her. Do you see how much of a joy, enlightenment or help your giftedness is to people?

Past encounters with family or other individuals where you were not allowed to be yourself may have created a sense of wanting to hide. Maybe you acquiesced to keep the peace, shrunk back instead of bursting forth. Well it's time to burst forth. Fully be the woman who God created and designed you to be. Your gifts and talents are needed. The apostle Paul told Timothy to fan the flame that's within him. What Paul was telling Timothy was to use his gifts. The things that burn inside need to be ignited. The more attention given to a fire, the bigger and brighter it shines. You are a light in this world, and when you cultivate your talents and share them with others, your fire kindles best.

God has a plan for you, and it's a good one! Get comfortable being you. Take deep breaths; hold them and let them out. Smile until your face hurts. Laugh until you cry. Dance until you're tired and can't move anymore. Your worth is beyond measure.

Not because I said it, but because Jesus sealed it. I want your entire life to be a party and a celebration of who God made you to be and all He has done for you and through you. Even if you can't see where you're going, that's okay. When you're at a party and your song comes on, get up and dance, and hope that the next song is one you can groove to as well. While you are in that moment, you're not thinking about what's next. You're living for the moment and dancing right now. Yesterday's jam is just that, it was the song of yesterday. Whatever tomorrow brings, you'll deal with it then. But today has a melody of its own, and that is what you celebrate and rock to right now.

You'll never get today, tomorrow. So, make the minutes count. Make up your mind that this is your season and time to show up as your best self. One of my mentors told me that I get to choose who I want to be, despite what anyone else does or says. I get to decide the woman I want to be and how I want to show up. I've taken this on fully. Whether I'm married or single, an entrepreneur or an employee, and whether someone is understanding or mean to me, my response is going to be the same. My response will be a reflection of true womanhood.

You and I we are daughters of the King, which means anything is possible. Jesus told us that He was glad to go to the Father, because greater works we would do with Holy Spirit once He left. This is your time of greatness, because it's the time that you're here on this Earth. Whether or not a man is in your life at the moment does not impact your purpose or significance.

A relationship status does not define you. Your value comes from God alone. And when you know who you really are, you're unstoppable. You are a movement. Celebrate!

Reflect

Love the Lord your God with all your heart and with all your soul and with all your mind and with all your strength.' The second is this: 'Love your neighbor as yourself.' There is no commandment greater than these." Mark 12:30 – 31 NIV

For I know the plans I have for you," says the LORD. "They are plans for good and not for disaster, to give you a future and a hope.

Jeremiah 29:11 NLT

What shall we say about such wonderful things as these? If God is for us, who can be against us?

Romans 8:31 NLT

That precious memory triggers another: your honest faith—and what a rich faith it is, handed down from your grandmother Lois to your mother Eunice, and now to you! And the special gift of ministry you received when I laid hands on you and prayed—keep that ablaze! God doesn't want us to be shy with his gifts, but bold and loving and sensible.

2 Timothy 1:5 - 7 MSG

- 10 -

Perspective

Life may not be a fairytale, but there is still room for magical moments. Romantic love is real and available for everyone. The good thing about a love story is that despite its highs and lows, it runs on a continuum. It's never too late to start loving and to embrace being loved. Perspective is everything. How do you view love and relationships? What's your vantage point?

Everyone has a different perspective. As the saying goes, "beauty is in the eye of the beholder." What are you choosing to behold? Do you choose to focus on the negative, or do you choose to focus on the positive? God says to not be conformed to the patterns of this world, but be transformed by the renewing of your mind so that He can show you what His good and acceptable will is. This world will tell you, and even your friends may tell you, that love doesn't exist. Some of my friends concur. They say there aren't any good men out there. If I entertain that conversation and line of thinking for too long, I may start to agree. However, my expectation is not based on this world's standards, but rather on God's. I'm not the only person and women are not the only gender with a Kingdom mindset. There are good men who have a Kingdom mindset. They have a heart, passion and love for God. Just like you desire to have love and be loved, there are brothers who want the same thing. They want to be a demonstration in this world of what God's love for the church looks like.

In the interim of meeting that person and cultivating a relationship, embrace the journey. It's one of exploration and discovery, fun and excitement. God gives us a full life and that doesn't start when you meet someone. If you don't believe it's possible or think that it will never happen for you, I challenge you to change your perspective. Be open to what may come; you might be surprised what you find, or who finds you, when you least expect it. Usually when I have misplaced something like my car keys or my cell phone, when I relax, go back to the area that I remember having it last, that is the moment that I find it, or it finds me. I walk into the kitchen and my head magically turns to the left to see the bread box. There lies my phone between the Texas toast and tortillas. I have no idea how it got there, but I found it where I least expected it to be. Sometimes that's how love comes, in unexpected shapes, forms and places.

I wish that I had an estimate for you, a timeline of when you'll meet "the one." But at the heart of the matter is trusting God. Trusting is not always easy, especially on those nights when it's cold and you want to cuddle. Or when you're doing something fun and want someone to share in that moment. Where is he on those nights when you hear a noise outside of your front door and you're afraid? How many times do you have to call AAA for a blown tire? It would be nice not to necessarily have a superhero but someone to be there, so you don't always have to wear that big "S" on *your* chest.

Know that you're not alone. There are millions of women out there desiring love and a lifelong, built-in best friend. There is a question mark as to whether or not they believe that good men exist. I want to ask a question. What would it take for you to believe that there's a good man out there, and there's one just for you? It may take going back and revisiting hurts, disappointments or abandonment. Processing through those things that have been tucked away, pinpointing believed mistruths and calling out those internal vows will start to change the mental narrative and perspective. There are counselors and community to help guide you through this process. And on the other side of the process is a more beautiful, resolved, resilient you.

I asked one of my besties if she believed that good men are out there. She said, "Based on what I've seen, I honestly don't know." I so admired and respected her candid answer. I asked her the question that I'm posing to you, "What would it take for you to believe?" She said, "It would take me really seeing and experiencing something completely different than I have before."

My friend is like a butterfly: bright, vibrant, unique. She is a beautiful blossom of a woman. She's been through a lot of things in life. Each one of those challenges has helped to transform her into someone even more beautiful on the other side. She's not the same coming out as she went in. And what she is attracted to now is much different than what she desired before. So when I look at her and we have conversations like these, I'm confident when I say, "You'll see something different. Your experience will be different."

If you so desire and are willing to be open to it, the people and subsequent relationships that will come will be less of the old and more of the new. There will be new dynamics and opportunities to foster friendships, which could grow into something so much more. We are God's daughters, and He loves us tremendously. He knows the things that we need and want. If one of those things is to be married and share life with someone, which is part of His design by the way. He'll make it happen. If you can't trust your experiences and it's challenging to trust the present because of what you see, then trust God. He can't fail; He doesn't lie; and He has good things for you. Be bold, tell Him what you desire. He'll exceed your expectations for sure. How many stories have you heard of women meeting someone who was out of this world amazing, and she had no idea where he came from? That sounds to me like a God send.

There's no expiration on blessedness. And though we don't always understand how God moves, this one thing is certain, when He does move it's swiftly, decisively and favorably. Queen, you are a divine treasure who would be a blessing to any man. You matter and your presence is visibly noted. Those who can't see clearly, God has only hidden you, because they are not for you. Good men do exist; they are not an endangered species. When the one comes, the timing will be perfect.

So how big is God to you? Is He larger than any problem? Is He able to introduce you to your mate? When God is magnified, a shift in perspective can occur. I was once fearful that I would be like many women in my family who got married, divorced and ended up raising kids alone. Many remained single, even after their children reached adulthood. This isn't something I desire for my life. Fear of ending up there stifled me in some of my choices and also in believing for God's best. I'd experienced first-hand abuse and adultery, as well as observed it in the lives of women that I love. But the history of others or even my own is not a predictor of the future. I had to ask myself, "How big is my God?"

Someone else's story isn't your story. And the story you've lived to this point does not have to be your future tale. When we put our life in God's hands, He completely takes over, because we've surrendered our will for His. It may feel as if you are blindly going into the future, because you don't know what the next step entails. But as you continue to walk with

God, each step feels more confident. Before you know it, you're striding and then leaping in faith. You know that everything's going to be okay. Yes, you may have been single for 10 years, or you're in your forties and not married. God is still faithful. That's your answer to those thoughts, feelings and questions of whether it will ever happen for you. Know that God is BIGGER than how it feels.

If God can create a world, design and fulfill His plan to redeem people with His life, could He not bring two individuals together? Is anything too hard for Him? He can work that thing out so that two people meet at 3 p.m. on the 25th of May, while one is going into Starbucks and the other is coming out. They bump into each other. The coffee and cake pops collide; there's a big mess. Initially, the feelings are anxiousness and irritation. Neither expected this hiccup or delay in their day. Yet as they finish brushing off the droplets of coffee, they look up and their eyes connect. Laughter erupts. God can orchestrate a meeting and cultivate chemistry in the most unique ways, even in the smallest of things.

Lean into God with your whole heart, mind, soul and strength. Don't worry about what it looks like, keep your focus on Him. The pages of your story are written, and God oversees it as you walk it out every day. Just because you don't know what is in the next paragraph or on the following page, doesn't mean He is not aware. Once you reach the resolve that God is big and He cares, life becomes colorful and exciting. Every day is an adventure and part of your never-ending story. It's time to release the doubt and shift your perspective. Forget the dismal outlook someone said about your future. Forget what the last guy did. It may take time and that's okay. But rehearse and meditate on what God says and what He has done. Wait expectedly to see what He is going to do. Perspective is everything. God says that as a man thinks in his heart, so is he. What are the beliefs that you treasure in your heart? If you believe you can't, most likely you won't. If you believe He can, assuredly He will.

Do I believe that they're good men? Absolutely! I rest on that, because God doesn't lie and that phenomenon will never occur. Even when somebody tries to approach me without good intentions, or if my closest friends are getting tons of dates and I can't remember the last time someone asked me my name or for my number, the truth still remains. Good men exist, because God made them and God is faithful. I know the monotony of dating can be discouraging, especially when there doesn't appear to be any potential prospects. Everyone's story is different. If I'm being hidden, it's for the right search and the perfect find.

Perspective. Perspective. Perspective. Do good men exist? Is there life still to be lived? Is purpose attached to your hope? Yes, yes and yes! What is your perspective? Did the hurt that you experienced at some point in your life seem insurmountable? Did you make it past that moment? What is your perspective? Have you ever laughed when you least expected? Have you ever received something you didn't plan for? Have you ever thought,

"Wow, I can't believe this is happening to me," in a good way? If you can say yes, then wow, doesn't that change your perspective?

It's not a hard reach when you reframe your mind. It's certainly not out of sight when you adjust your focus. You are a daughter and a queen. And your Father has good things in store for you. Know that. Trust that. And you will see that good man who is after God's heart. God's first assessment of man when He created him was that man was good, very good. And His sons still are. Enjoy the process; embrace the journey. Love and grow who you are in Christ. As you pursue purpose, your path will meet with the one who's purposed for you. So live life on purpose, and never lose hope or perspective.

Reflect

Stop imitating the ideals and opinions of the culture around you,[a] but be inwardly transformed by the Holy Spirit through a total reformation of how you think. This will empower you to discern God's will as you live a beautiful life, satisfying and perfect in his eyes.

Romans 12:2 TPT

Two are better than one, because they have a good return for their labor: If either of them falls down, one can help the other up.

But pity anyone who falls and has no one to help them up. Also, if two lie down together, they will keep warm. But how can one keep warm alone? Though one may be overpowered, two can defend themselves. A cord of three strands is not quickly broken.

Ecclesiastes 4:9-12 NIV

www.ingramcontent.com/pod-product-compliance
Lightning Source LLC
LaVergne TN
LVHW020633100826
845148LV00012B/2162

* 9 7 8 0 5 7 8 9 4 7 6 2 4 *